THE SHOOTING SCRIPT®

THE SQUID AND THE WHALE

THE SQUID AND THE WHALE

SCREENPLAY BY
NOAH BAUMBACH

INTRODUCTION BY WES ANDERSON
Q&A WITH NOAH BAUMBACH

A Newmarket Shooting Script® Series Book
NEWMARKET PRESS • NEW YORK

For Mannie

FIRST EDITION

ISBN: 1-55704-700-6

10   9   8   7   6   5   4   3   2

Library of Congress Cataloging-in-Publication Data

Baumbach, Noah, 1969-
The squid and the whale : the shooting script / screenplay by Noah Baumbach ;
introduction by Wes Anderson. —1st ed.
p. cm.
Includes bibliographical references.
ISBN 1-55704-700-6 (pbk. : alk. paper)
I. Squid and the whale (Motion picture) II. Title.
PN1997.2.S697 2005
791.43'72—dc22

2005025590

QUANTITY PURCHASES

Companies, professional groups, clubs, and other organizations may qualify for special terms when ordering quantities
of this title. For information, write to Special Sales Department, Newmarket Press, 18 East 48th Street, New York, NY
10017; call (212) 832-3575; FAX (212) 832-3629; or e-mail info@newmarketpress.com.

www.newmarketpress.com

Manufactured in the United States of America.

OTHER BOOKS IN THE NEWMARKET SHOOTING SCRIPT® SERIES INCLUDE:

About a Boy: The Shooting Script
Adaptation: The Shooting Script
The Age of Innocence: The Shooting Script
American Beauty: The Shooting Script
Ararat: The Shooting Script
A Beautiful Mind: The Shooting Script
Big Fish: The Shooting Script
The Birdcage: The Shooting Script
Blackhawk Down: The Shooting Script
Cast Away: The Shooting Script
Cinderella Man: The Shooting Script
Dead Man Walking: The Shooting Script
Dreamcatcher: The Shooting Script
Erin Brockovich: The Shooting Script
Eternal Sunshine of the Spotless Mind:
    The Shooting Script
Gods and Monsters: The Shooting Script
Gosford Park: The Shooting Script
Human Nature: The Shooting Script
I ♥ Huckabees: The Shooting Script
The Ice Storm: The Shooting Script

Igby Goes Down: The Shooting Script
In Good Company: The Shooting Script
Knight's Tale: The Shooting Script
Man on the Moon: The Shooting Script
The Matrix: The Shooting Script
Nurse Betty: The Shooting Script
Pieces of April: The Shooting Script
The People vs. Larry Flynt: The Shooting Script
Punch-Drunk Love: The Shooting Script
Red Dragon: The Shooting Script
The Shawshank Redemption: The Shooting Script
Sideways: The Shooting Script
Snatch: The Shooting Script
Snow Falling on Cedars: The Shooting Script
Spanglish: The Shooting Script
State and Main: The Shooting Script
Sylvia: The Shooting Script
Traffic: The Shooting Script
The Truman Show: The Shooting Script
U-Turn: The Shooting Script
War of the Worlds: The Shooting Script

CONTENTS

Introduction by Wes Anderson   vii

The Shooting Script   1

Photo insert following page   86

Scene Notes by Noah Baumbach   113

Q & A with Noah Baumbach   119

Cast and Crew Credits   130

About the Filmmakers   134

INTRODUCTION

BY WES ANDERSON

One night five years ago, my ex-girlfriend Jennifer and I had dinner with Noah Baumbach and his younger brother Nico at an Italian restaurant on the Upper East Side called Primola. I had already known Noah a couple of years. We saw each other frequently, always for dinner. There was a famous baseball player for the Mets, Rusty Staub, in the room that night. Noah said to Nico, "We should get his autograph for Dad." Nico agreed, "We should." Neither of the brothers gave any indication that he was going to actually try to accomplish this, but something had been triggered. They exchanged a few mysterious remarks and laughed. They drifted into a quiet discussion and then included us: they were talking about their father. They talked about joint custody, veal cutlets, Norman Mailer's agent—the events of their childhood and of "The Squid and the Whale." Noah told the stories, animated and energetic as he always is when he captures an audience and gets them laughing. Nico periodically interjected his own brief, deadpan details. We all listened through three courses. At the end of it, we were silent, as if a curtain had fallen. We ordered coffee, and I said, feeling smart, "*That's* the movie you should make." Noah said, "I'm working on it," which it then occurred to me was pretty obvious. He is a writer and had clearly given the matter some thought. I said,

"Well, I want to get in on this one," and I did. I think the end result is his funniest, saddest, most honest film.

As we left the restaurant, Jennifer stopped at Rusty Staub's table and sweetly collected his autograph for Mr. Baumbach. I had hoped to reproduce it below, but Noah has informed me that his father accidentally threw it out with the wrapping paper over Christmas.

—September 2005

THE SQUID AND THE WHALE

by

Noah Baumbach

BLACK

                    FRANK (V.O.)
          Mom and me versus you and Dad.

1   INT. TENNIS COURTS - DAY   1

A big tent-like bubble. About eight courts. Mostly empty.
An older couple plays on 2. On 5, BERNARD BERKMAN, late
40's, and WALT BERKMAN, 16, play against JOAN BERKMAN, late
30's, and FRANK BERKMAN, 12. Frank, who's skilled for his
age, serves a bullet.

                    BERNARD
          Long!

                    FRANK
          That looked pretty good.

                    BERNARD
          It was out.

                    JOAN
               (for Frank's benefit)
          It did look good.

                    WALT
          Frank, it was out!

                    BERNARD
          It's my call. Out!

Frank looks back in disbelief.

                    BERNARD (CONT'D)
               (aside to Walt)
          If you can, try and hit at your mother's
          backhand, it's pretty weak.

                    WALT
          Got it.

Frank serves a soft second serve which Walt smacks to Joan's
backhand. She can't return it.

                    WALT (CONT'D)
          Yes!

                    JOAN
          Don't gloat, Walt.

                                              (CONTINUED)

Frank tosses the balls back over the net to Bernard.

                         BERNARD
               5 games to 3, us.

Bernard, clearly self-taught but effective, serves into the
net.

                         BERNARD (CONT'D)
               Fuck! Come on, Bernard.

                         JOAN
               Bernard, don't curse!

                         BERNARD
               I'm cursing at myself.

Bernard serves. Frank returns it. Walt volleys at his
mother's head. She ducks. It's in.

                         BERNARD (CONT'D)
               Nice shot.

                         WALT
               Thanks.

                         JOAN
                    (growing tense)
               Watch out, Walt.

                         WALT
               It's part of the game, Mom.

Bernard serves. Joan returns it. Bernard hits an approach
shot and goes to the net. Joan hits a weak lob and Bernard
smashes it. The ball smacks off Joan's back and sails onto
another court. Bernard laughs.

                         WALT (CONT'D)
               Yes!

Joan, disgusted, drops her racquet and walks off the court.

                         BERNARD
               Joan! I'm sorry! It was an accident!

Bernard goes after her. Frank and Walt approach the net.
They watch Bernard and Joan talk over by the entrance.

(CONTINUED)

                              WALT
                    (shakes his head, smiling)
                You got to get a second serve.

Joan, angrily, walks out leaving Bernard behind. Bernard
waves for the kids to follow. Both the boys groan.

2   INT/EXT. THE BERKMAN'S PEUGEOT - DUSK   2

     TITLE:

                    Park Slope, Brooklyn, New York
                                1986

Bernard drives an old maroon Peugeot. Joan in the passenger
seat. In the back, Walt listens to his Walkman as he pulls
on a loose string on the back of his father's seat. Frank
reads a book on the Galapagos Islands.

3   INT. FRANK'S ROOM - NIGHT   3

Frank drinks mouthwash, gargles and swallows it. He
readjusts the position of a ceramic turtle on a shelf full of
different size turtles. His walls are covered with posters
of Vitas Gerulitas, Arthur Ashe and pictures of animals from
the Galapagos Island. He climbs into bed. Joan sits beside
him.

                              FRANK
                Did Dad hit you on purpose?

                              JOAN
                No, he wouldn't do that, but he got too
                caught up in the game.

                              FRANK
                It felt on purpose.

                              JOAN
                    (pause)
                I know what you mean. But it wasn't.

They both say nothing for a moment.

                              FRANK
                Are you getting a divorce? You promised
                when we were in New Hampshire you and Dad
                would always be married.

                                                          (CONTINUED)

3   CONTINUED:

                         JOAN
              Which New Hampshire?

                         FRANK
              The one where the cat got caught in the
              radiator.

                         JOAN
              I don't remember.

                         FRANK
              You did. I asked you when we were in New
              Hampshire and you promised.

Joan studies his face.

                         JOAN
              Did I? Hmm.

                         FRANK
                    (pause)
              Do the ant with the iron boots.

                         JOAN
              Okay, but you're getting too old for
              that.

She takes his bare foot and walks with her fingernails across
its bottom.

                         JOAN (CONT'D)
              Here comes the ant with the iron boots.

Frank's face clenches, both loving and hating the ticklishness.

4   INT. BROOKLYN HOUSE - NIGHT   4

A party. Kids gather in clusters. Walt and his buddies,
LANCE and JEFFREY, 16, hang out by the window. Walt lectures:

                         WALT
              It's Welles' masterpiece, really. Many
              people think it's Citizen Kane, but
              Magnificent Ambersons, if it hadn't been
              ruined by the studio, would've been his
              crowning achievement. As it is, it's
              still brilliant. It's the old story,
              genius not being recognized by the
              industry.

(CONTINUED)

4   CONTINUED:

                          LANCE
          It sounds great. Who's in it?

                          WALT
             (pause)
          Orson Welles? I don't know, I haven't
          seen it yet. I've seen stills.
             (confidence returning)
          My Dad turned me on to it.

They watch SOPHIE GREENBERG, 17, who is probably going to be
quite pretty, but hasn't gotten there yet, across the room
talking to her friends.

                          JEFFREY
          Sophie's looking good.

                          LANCE
          Walt, I heard she likes you.

                          WALT
          She's kind of cute.

                          JEFFREY
          Very cute.

                          WALT
          Yeah, she's cute. She's not gorgeous,
          though. She's not Kate Roache cute.

KATE ROACHE, 16, one of those girls who got real pretty real
fast, talks to a group of boys.

                          LANCE
          No, but who is? I mean, besides Kate
          Roache. And Kate just likes college
          assholes.

                          JEFFREY
          Dicks. She's a whore.

OTTO, 16, their other friend approaches. Lance holds out his
finger like it's radar and picking up a signal coming from
Otto. He beeps quicker and quicker.

                          LANCE
          Ooh, my loser detector is going
          off...beep...beep...beep...beep...

Otto is clearly used to this, but still annoyed.

                                                    (CONTINUED)

4   CONTINUED: (2)

                         OTTO
          Okay, enough.

                         LANCE
          You know Otto's never jerked off.

                         WALT
          Really?

                         OTTO
          Thanks, Lance. Last time I confide in
          you at a sleepover.

                         JEFFREY
          Why wouldn't you jerk off?

                         OTTO
          Never occurred to me.

                         WALT
          You think Sophie's cute enough?

                         JEFFREY
          For what?

                         WALT
          To be my girlfriend.

                         JEFFREY
          Yeah, why not?

                         LANCE
          I heard she took her shirt off for Nelson
          Barton over break.

                         WALT
          Really? He's an ass. Isn't she a
          senior, she'll be leaving for college.

                         LANCE
          You don't have to marry her.

                         JEFFREY
          Just fuck her. Fuck her ass. With your
          cock.

They both look at Jeffrey, taken aback.

                         WALT
          Jesus.

                                              (CONTINUED)

4   CONTINUED: (3)   4

Sophie looks in Walt's direction. He looks away, then looks
back and she's no longer looking.

5   OMITTED   5

6   INT. BERKMAN LIVING ROOM - MORNING   6

Frank walks down the stairs, ready for school. Bernard is
folding up the couch, trying to do it quickly.

                         FRANK
              What are you doing?

                         BERNARD
              Just fixing up the couch.

                         FRANK
              Did you sleep there?

                         BERNARD
                   (pause)
              Yeah, our bed is hurting my back.

                         FRANK
              Isn't the couch worse than the bed? For
              backs?

                         BERNARD
              No. This...this is better.

7   EXT. BROOKLYN STREET - MORNING   7

Walt walks Frank to school. They both carry their bookbags.

                         FRANK
              When does Mom's story come out in the
              magazine?

                         WALT
              It's not a magazine, it's a literary
              journal. Next month, I think.

                         FRANK
              It'll be weird having two writers as
              parents.

                         WALT
              Well...Dad influenced her. She never
              wrote before she met him.

                                                  (CONTINUED)

7   CONTINUED:

                    FRANK
I haven't read any of Dad's books.

                    WALT
I've looked at them. They're great.
Very dense. I think he needs a new
agent. It's been too long since his last
book. The publishing world isn't
receptive always to real literary talent.

                    FRANK
Maybe Mom will be famous instead.

                    WALT
Dad's the writer.

                    FRANK
But maybe Mom's better.

                    WALT
That's way off base, Frank. Way off
base.

8   INT. HIGHSCHOOL HALLWAY - DAY   8

INSERT: A sign-up sheet written in three colors of magic
marker on poster board tacked up on a bulletin board. It
reads: "CAN YOU DO SOMETHING NO ONE ELSE CAN? PROVE IT AT THE
ANNUAL MIDWOOD HIGH TALENT SHOW. BE THERE OR BE RECTANGULAR."

A rectangle made of yarn is glued to the bottom of the sign.

Walt and another kid, TONY study the poster.

                    WALT
What are you gonna do, Tony?

                    TONY
Puppets. I make my own puppets and
perform these rather elaborate and
innovative narratives that I invent for
them. Yourself?

                    WALT
                  (shrugs)
I think I might just do a song on guitar.

9   INT. TENNIS COURTS - DAY   9

The bubble. Frank, in his mismatched whites, serves to the
instructor, IVAN, late 30's. CARL, 12, waits his turn at the
baseline. Bernard watches from the sidelines.

                    FRANK
          Ivan hit with Arthur Ashe once.

                    CARL
          Wasn't he ranked like four hundred and
          two or something?

                    FRANK
          Two hundred and sixty-eight. He said
          Ashe was a gentleman and thanked Ivan
          after they hit. Ivan could've been a
          champion if he hadn't hurt his knee.

Ivan jogs to the net.

                    IVAN
          Okay, brother, let's see some ground
          strokes.

Ivan volleys to Frank who smacks a bullet way out.

                    IVAN (CONT'D)
          You gotta ease up there, my brother.
          Jimmy Connors hits everything as hard as
          he can, but we can't all get away with
          that. Let's see a backhand.

Frank tries his weak, flat one handed backhand.

                    IVAN (CONT'D)
          Two hands. My brother, who taught you
          these junkyard strokes?

                    FRANK
          My Dad. He's self-taught.

                    IVAN
          I heard that. Well, we're gonna have to
          undo some of this damage.

                    FRANK
          He won't like that.

                                          (CONTINUED)

9   CONTINUED:

                    IVAN
          Hey, Bernard, you teaching my brother
          junkyard chip shots?

Bernard perks up and jogs onto the court.

                    BERNARD
          A one handed backhand is an elegant
          stroke.

                    IVAN
          My brother doesn't want a weak chip shot
          for a backhand.

                    FRANK
          I don't care.

                    BERNARD
          It's McEnroe's stroke. He's a master of
          the chip game.

Ivan shrugs, checks his watch and turns to the boys.

                    IVAN
          Okay, my brothers, that's it for today.

                    BERNARD
          Ivan, you want to hit a little?

                    IVAN
          I got a few minutes.

                    BERNARD
          Frank, you and Carl hang out. Give me
          your racquet.

CUT TO:

Bernard holds Frank's junior racquet and, in his street clothes,
waits at the baseline. He dabs his forehead with Frank's single
wristband. They begin. Ivan has fluid strokes, Bernard his
awkward slices. There's a palpable tension as the two men hit,
Bernard playing full out. Frank and Carl watch, impressed
Bernard can hold his own. Bernard hits a slice backhand down the
line and approaches the net. Ivan puts it away.

10   INT/EXT. BERNARD'S PEUGEOT - DUSK   10

Bernard drives, having sweated through his shirt and pants.
Frank, in the front seat.

                                              (CONTINUED)

> BERNARD
> Are you interested in any arts?

> FRANK
> I wouldn't mind being a pro.

> BERNARD
> It's very hard to be a professional
> player. As good as even someone like
> Ivan is, he isn't in a league with
> McEnroe or Connors.

> FRANK
> I don't mean a pro like that. I mean,
> like a pro at the bubble. Like Ivan.

> BERNARD
> You don't want to be a pro.
>   (pause)
> I'm sure I lost my parking space so we're
> gonna have to drive around.

> FRANK
> Can you drop me off?

> BERNARD
> No. I picked you up, the least you can
> do is ride around with me.

> FRANK
>   (resigned)
> Okay.

11   INT. WALT'S ROOM - NIGHT   11

We START on the record sleeve of Pink Floyd's "The Wall" and
MOVE to the sheet music for the song, "Hey You". We CONTINUE
up to Walt, who sits crosslegged, headphones on, playing
along on guitar.

12   INT. LIVING ROOM - NIGHT   12

Bernard and Joan sit on the couch watching as Walt plays and
sings the same Pink Floyd song. Frank sings back up.

> WALT
>   "Hey you. Out there in the cold..."

The boys finish the song. Bernard and Joan applaud.

(CONTINUED)

12   CONTINUED:

                         JOAN
              Terrific, honeys!

                         BERNARD
              Walt, did you write that song?

                         WALT
              Yes.

Frank looks at Walt, surprised.

                         WALT (CONT'D)
              Frank had some good ideas too.

Joan smiles at Frank. He shrugs modestly, but confused.

                         BERNARD
              Very dense. Very interesting.

                         WALT
              Yeah. I signed up for the talent thing
              they have at school.

                         JOAN
                   (suddenly stern)
              Great. Make sure you practice a lot.

                         WALT
                   (annoyed)
              Mom...I'll be fine.

                         JOAN
              Just remember, you'll be in front of a
              lot of people.

                         WALT
              Mom, don't ruin the whole thing for me.

                         BERNARD
              You'll win. If you don't win, something's
              wrong with them -- which is probably the
              case actually. People can be very stupid.

The phone rings. Joan, in an overly casual gesture, stands
and walks tightly, but briskly into the kitchen.

                         JOAN
              I'll get it.

Bernard watches her disappear.

                                          (CONTINUED)

                              BERNARD
          Walt, would you like to come to my class
          tomorrow after school?

                              WALT
          Yeah.

                              FRANK
          Could I come?

                              BERNARD
          You have tennis.
              (pause)
          You're going to be doing that which is
          its own thing.

A muffled "Hello" from the other room, some hushed
conversation. Bernard still looks in Joan's direction,
trying to make out what she's saying, his face darkening.

                              FRANK
          Look how young Dad looks.

Frank holds a copy of Under Water a novel by Bernard Berkman.
He shows Walt the photo of their Dad on the back of the book.

                              WALT
          That's funny.

They laugh. Bernard's eyes remain fixed on the kitchen.

                              WALT (CONT'D)
          Dad, can I have this?

                              BERNARD
          Okay.

                              WALT
          Would you write something in it?

Bernard, distracted, opens the book, scribbles "Best Wishes"
and his signature. A moment, then he reconsiders and writes
"Dad" in parentheses. Walt examines it, smiles, and says
cheerily:

                              WALT (CONT'D)
          Thanks.

13   INT. BROOKLYN COLLEGE CLASSROOM - DAY   13

Bernard sits around a table with fifteen GRADUATE STUDENTS.
Walt sits there as well. LILI THORN, 24, reads her story.

                    LILI
          "I absorb sex indiscriminately, numb and
          impartial. I suck men of their
          interiors, a fuck that unites John, Dan,
          Scott, Whomever. In the popular lust and
          paternal hunt for my possession..."

We MOVE around the room of students, who mostly listen
politely or with vague interest. One is a burly, curly haired
GUY who stares intently at Lili, but doesn't appear to be
listening. Walt is fascinated. Bernard watches, also very
interested.

14   INT/EXT. BERNARD'S PEUGEOT - DUSK   14

Bernard drives, in a bright mood. Walt in the seat next to him.

                    BERNARD
          She's a very risky writer, Lili. Very
          racy. I mean, exhibiting her cunt in
          that fashion is very racy. I mean Lili
          has her influences in post modern
          literature, it's a bit derivative of
          Kafka, but for a student, very racy. Did
          you get that it was her cunt?

                    WALT
          Oh, yeah.

                    BERNARD
          Did you like it?

                    WALT
          Yeah. A lot.

                    BERNARD
          You'd like Kafka. One of my
          predecessors. Particularly The
          Metamorphosis.

                    WALT
               (committing to memory)
          The Metamorphosis.

Bernard turns the car onto their block.

                                              (CONTINUED)

                              BERNARD
                    No fucking spaces.

                              WALT
                    I'll keep you company while we look.

                              BERNARD
                    Thank you.

                              WALT
                    Dad, what were your wives like before
                    Mom?

                              BERNARD
                    Wife really. The first one was annulled.
                    I was nineteen.

                              WALT
                    What was she like?

                              BERNARD
                    The annulled one?

                              WALT
                    No, the one you'd call a wife.

                              BERNARD
                         (thinks)
                    Difficult.

The car turns the corner. Joan and a MAN are talking very
close. Walt cranes his neck to get a better look. Bernard
sees this too.

                              WALT
                    That's Mom.

                              BERNARD
                         (blankly)
                    Yeah, that's mom.

They keep driving.

                              BERNARD (CONT'D)
                         (pause, to himself)
                    What was she wearing? No, I guess I've
                    seen that before.

Neither of them says anything. Bernard hits the blinker.

15   INT. DINING ROOM - NIGHT   15

The family eats in silence. Walt makes quick eye contact
with his mother who smiles warmly at him. He doesn't smile
back. Bernard looks distracted, upset. Frank takes a nut
off his plate and puts it up his nose.

                    JOAN
          Frank! Did you just put that peanut up
          your nose?

                    FRANK
               (pause)
          Cashew. Yes.

He tries to blow it out, but to no avail. He looks at his
mother, unsure of what to do.

                    JOAN
          Oh, pickle. That's just an idiotic,
          stupid thing to do. That peanut can kill
          you.

Frank acts like he got it out.

                    FRANK
          No, it's out. I got it.

But he didn't. Walt gives Frank a look, turns to his Dad.

                    WALT
          We're reading A Tale of Two Cities in
          English. Is that any good?

                    BERNARD
          It's minor Dickens. Popular in schools,
          but I think David Copperfield or Great
          Expectations is much richer. What is it
          about highschool that you read all the
          worst books by good writers?

                    JOAN
          You should read it yourself and see what
          you think of it.

                    WALT
               (curtly)
          I don't wanna waste my time.

Joan is surprised by this. Walt doesn't look up.

16   INT. LIVING ROOM - NIGHT   16

Bernard is arranging the pull-out couch for bed. A click,
click, click is coming from the other room. He places a
glass of water and his watch by the bedside and goes into:

17   INT. DINING ROOM - CONTINUOUS   17

Joan is typing at the dining room table. Bernard stops in
the doorway and watches. He looks at her with silent
resentment.

                    BERNARD
          What are you writing?

                    JOAN
          I'm working on the Peugeot story.

                    BERNARD
          Did you take my note about the ending?

                    JOAN
          Some of it.

                    BERNARD
          Does he still die?

                    JOAN
          Yeah.

                    BERNARD
          Then you didn't take my note.

The phone rings. They both look at it. A pause and Joan
answers it.

                    JOAN
          Hello?...Hi...

She looks at Bernard awkwardly. Suddenly he charges at her,
grabs the phone and slams it down.

18   INT. FRANK'S ROOM - NIGHT   18

The distant sound of yelling. Frank rolls over in bed,
trying not to listen. He tries to breathe out of his
nostril, the cashew still lodged up there.

19   INT. WALT'S ROOM/HALLWAY - NIGHT   19

Walt, sitting up in bed, is trying to hear. His father
yells, "You're making me crazy!". Walt gets up and walks
down the hallway. He lies down at the top of the stairs and
listens.

20   INT. BERKMAN LIVING ROOM - MORNING   20

Walt and Frank are putting on their coats, packing bookbags.
Bernard stands in the doorway.

                    BERNARD
          Umm, boys, make sure you come home right
          after school.

                    FRANK
          Why?

                    BERNARD
          We're having a family conference.

                    WALT
          What's that?

                    BERNARD
          A talk. Just come home.

                    WALT
          What about?

                    BERNARD
          We'll go over it tonight.

                    WALT
          Can't you give us a hint?

                    BERNARD
               (flustered)
          No, just...tonight, we'll go over
          everything.

21   EXT. BROOKLYN STREET - MORNING   21

Walt and Frank walk in silence, both looking anxious. Walt
drops Frank off at his school.

22   INT. SUBWAY - MORNING   22

Walt sits, a blank look on his face.

23   INT. JUNIOR HIGHSCHOOL LIBRARY - DAY   23

Frank sits with Carl at a table. Carl talks incessantly,
Frank does not respond.

24   EXT. BROOKLYN STREET - LATE DAY   24

Same spot. Frank is waiting as Walt picks him up. They
start home together, just as anxious and silent. They do not
speak, even to say, Hello.

25   INT. BERKMAN LIVING ROOM - DUSK   25

Frank and Walt sit in front of Bernard in an oddly formal
manner.

                BERNARD
     Just waiting for your mother.

The toilet flushes and Joan comes out of the bathroom and
joins them. The boys hold their noses.

                WALT
     Oh, mom.

                JOAN
     Sorry. Okay.

                BERNARD
     Okay. All set?

                JOAN
     Yes.

                BERNARD
     Okay, your mom and I...

Anticipating what's coming, Frank just bursts into tears.

                BERNARD (CONT'D)
     Okay...yeah...Mom and I are going...
         (off Frank's tears)
     Yeah...we're going to separate.

Frank puts his head in his hands, crying harder. Walt looks
at his brother and back at his Mom who smiles at him. He
doesn't know what to say.

                        (CONTINUED)

                    JOAN
You're not going to be leaving either of
us.

                    BERNARD
          (like it's a great opportunity)
We're gonna have joint custody...Frank,
it's okay. I've got an elegant new house
across the park.

                    FRANK
Across the park! That's so far away. Is
that even Brooklyn?

                    BERNARD
It's only five stops on the subway from
here. It's an elegant block. The filet
of the neighborhood.
          (smiling at Walt)
We'll have a ping pong table.

                    WALT
I don't play ping pong.

                    JOAN
And we'll both see you equally.

                    WALT
How will that work?

                    BERNARD
We're splitting up the week. Alternating
days.

                    FRANK
Why?

                    BERNARD
Cause I love you and want to see you as
much as your mother does.

                    WALT
But there's seven days.

                    BERNARD
Right.

                    WALT
How will you split evenly with seven
days?

                         BERNARD
              Oh, I got you Tuesday, Wednesday and
              Saturday. And every other Thursday.

                         FRANK
                    (crying)
              Every other?

                         BERNARD
              That's how we each have you equally.

                         JOAN
              That was your father's idea.

                         FRANK
                    (sobbing)
              Don't do this.

                         WALT
              How will I get to school?

                         BERNARD
              There's a subway four blocks from the
              house. Four or five. No more than six
              blocks.

                         WALT
              What about the cat?

The CAT, a fat furry thing, watches from the archway.

                         JOAN
              Shit, the cat.

                         BERNARD
              We didn't discuss the cat.

Bernard looks at Joan, who is waiting for him to answer.

                         JOAN
              Your father will pick him up on those
              days when you're switching houses.

                         BERNARD
                    (annoyed)
              I'll have to drive here two additional
              times a week?

                    JOAN
          I guess so. You got a place on the other
          side of the park. If you'd gotten a place
          near here, it wouldn't be a problem.

                    BERNARD
          This neighborhood has gotten very
          expensive. Joan, it's very painful for
          me to stay in this neighborhood, you know
          that. Don't be difficult. I feel
          banished.

Frank starts crying again.

                    JOAN
          Oh, pickle...

                    WALT
          So, Dad, what will happen with the cat?
               (realizing)
          And my guitar. Who will transfer my
          guitar?

                    BERNARD
               (muttering)
          We'll figure something out.

26   INT. BERKMAN BATHROOM - NIGHT   26

Joan brushes her teeth. She turns and is startled to see
Walt in the doorway. He's very grave.

                    WALT
          Is it cause Dad isn't as successful as he
          used to be?

Joan says nothing. She spits into the sink.

                    WALT (CONT'D)
          Now that you're publishing and he--

                    JOAN
          Walt, that's not a nice thing to say.

                    WALT
          Because this is a great family and I
          don't know why you're screwing it up.

                    JOAN
          If we could avoid it, I would.

                                              (CONTINUED)

> WALT
> Why are you doing this <u>now</u>? You've been
> together sixteen years--

> JOAN
> Seventeen.

> WALT
> I can't imagine living with you guys like
> this.

> JOAN
> Don't most of your friends already have
> divorced parents?

> WALT
> Yeah, but <u>I</u> don't.

Joan's face has a light sheen of sweat. She buries her face
in a towel for a moment. She resurfaces and locks eyes with
her son.

> JOAN
> Well, now you do.

> WALT
> I think you're doing a foolish, foolish
> thing.

> JOAN
> Listen, chicken, I understand how unhappy
> you are. I'm unhappy too. And I don't
> want you or Frank to blame yourself for
> any of this.
>   (direct)
> It has nothing to do with you.

Walt, flustered, walks into his room.

Joan looks at herself in the mirror. She leans in, her lips
are very dry. She takes a loose piece of chapped skin and
tears it from her lip. It starts to bleed.

27   INT. BERKMAN LIVING ROOM - NIGHT   27

Bernard sleeps on the pull-out couch. Joan quietly walks by
with a stack of books in her arms.

28   INT. FRANK'S ROOM - NIGHT   28

Frank wakes up with a start.

                    FRANK
            Woa, woa...

He looks down at his feet. Joan is sliding books under his
bed.

                    JOAN
            Shh. It's okay, go back to sleep.

                    FRANK
                (pause)
            Are those books?

                    JOAN
            Yes. These are my books.

                    FRANK
            Why are they going under the bed?

                    JOAN
            Because I bought them and I don't want to
            lose them.

Joan sits down on the floor crosslegged. She sighs and says
to herself.

                    JOAN (CONT'D)
            We'll put them back on the shelf when
            your father leaves.

29   EXT. BROOKLYN STREET - MORNING   29

Walt and Frank walk to school in silence. Frank's eyes are
red and puffy from crying. Walt stays cool.

                    WALT
            Until things are certain I don't think we
            should say anything to anyone yet.

                    FRANK
                Why?

                    WALT
            Cause we never know and I don't want
            people to know our business.

                                                    (CONTINUED)

29   CONTINUED: 29

                         FRANK
              I told Carl.

                         WALT
              Already?

                         FRANK
              I called him last night. I also told
              Matt and Dale.

Frank bursts into tears just thinking about it.

                         WALT
              And Dale. Shit, now everyone will know.
              Jesus, Frank.

                         FRANK
              Mom says we should tell people.

                         WALT
              Mom doesn't have to go to school. Stop
              crying.

Frank takes off for his school. Walt, dismissively, waves
him off and heads for the subway.

30   EXT. SUBWAY PLATFORM - MORNING   30

Walt, Jeffrey, Otto and Lance exit the train. Walt wants to
say something, but doesn't know how to say it. The others
are a bit stilted as well, aware that something is up.

                         LANCE
              I constantly get a boner on the D train.

                         JEFFREY
              Just the D?

                         LANCE
              Other trains too. Bus sometimes. New
              York transportation pretty much does it.

                         WALT
              My parents are divorcing.

The boys all kind of mumble, nod.

                         WALT (CONT'D)
              I figured you all might know already, but
              that's...anyway, it sort of sucks.

(CONTINUED)

CONTINUED:

More mumbling, agreeing. Otto turns to Walt.

                    OTTO
          I heard it's joint custody. Joint
          custody blows.

                    WALT
          I was told it's better.

                    OTTO
          It's miserable. My parents didn't want
          to uproot me and Rebecca so we stayed in
          the house and they both took separate
          apartments and switched off coming to us.
          Then my Mom met Dexter, and my Dad
          freaked out. And then they sold the
          house and I go back and forth anyway.
          Joint custody blows.

A train rumbles into the station. CUT TO BLACK.

31   INT./EXT. BERNARD'S PEUGEOT - DUSK   31

Bernard pulls up in front of the Jewish Community Center.
Walt, in a mismatched jacket and tie, is buckled in next to
him.

                    BERNARD
          I'm gonna take you guys to see my new
          house next week. It'll be nice to move
          in finally, that couch is killing my
          back.

                    WALT
               (nods)
          Could I have some money?

                    BERNARD
          For what?

                    WALT
          To get something to eat after class.

                    BERNARD
          Here.

He digs in his wallet and produces two dollars. Walt frowns.

                    BERNARD (CONT'D)
          What?

                                                       (CONTINUED)

31   CONTINUED: 31

                    WALT
          Two dollars won't get me a plate of
          fries.

                    BERNARD
          How much is a plate of fries?

                    WALT
          I don't know. Four dollars?

                    BERNARD
          For fries?

Bernard, incredulous, goes into his pockets. He trickles
some change into Walt's hand. Walt says nothing. Walt
climbs out of the car, shuts the door. Turns to the Center
and then back at his Dad. They meet eyes for a second and
Walt waves, but Bernard has turned away, missing the gesture.

                    DANCE TEACHER (O.S.)
          Okay, rotate.

32   INT. JEWISH COMMUNITY CENTER - DUSK   32

A circle of girls and a rotating circle of boys. Most kids
in clashing, odd formal wear. Each boy dances a dance with a
girl and then moves on to the next girl. Walt moves over to
Sophie.

                    SOPHIE
          You live in Park Slope, right?

                    WALT
          My mom does...and I do sometimes.

                    DANCE TEACHER
          Side, step, back step, side, step, back
          step...

                    WALT
          I'm also going to live on the other side
          of the park. Half the time.

                    SOPHIE
          Prospect Heights?

                    WALT
          I don't know what the neighborhood's
          called actually. The street's Stratford
          Road. My Dad's moving there.

                                                    (CONTINUED)

32   CONTINUED:

                         SOPHIE
          I know Stratford. What number on
          Stratford?

                         WALT
          Umm...three something maybe...I'm not
          sure actually. I haven't seen it yet. I
          hear it's the filet of the neighborhood.

Sophie nods, unsure what that means. They dance.

                         WALT (CONT'D)
          You like Franz Kafka?

                         SOPHIE
          I don't know him.

                         WALT
          He's great. The Metamorphosis is a
          masterpiece.

                         SOPHIE
          Sounds good.

                         WALT
          It is.

                         SOPHIE
          Have you read This Side of Paradise?

                         WALT
          No, but it's minor Fitzgerald.

                         SOPHIE
          Is it? I loved it.

                         WALT
          It's a minor work. Gatsby's his
          masterpiece and Tender Is The Night has
          dazzling moments, Last Tycoon, had he
          finished it--

                         DANCE TEACHER
          Shhh!

Walt makes a face to Sophie and they laugh.

33   INT/EXT. BERNARD'S PEUGEOT - DAY   33

Bernard waits outside Joan's house. He keeps the car
running, tensely clutching the wheel. He opens the glove
compartment, takes out a mix tape made by Walt and puts it in
the tape deck. He puts his hands back on the wheel.
Finally, Walt and Frank come out the front door. Frank holds
the cat under his arm.

34   INT. BERNARD'S PEUGEOT - DAY   34

They drive. Walt goes into his bag and takes out a couple of
books, Dostoyevsky, Melville, and hands them to Bernard.

                    BERNARD
          Oh, thanks. Yeah, I forgot to take
          these. She has a few of my books still.
          She went around writing her maiden name
          in all the books once she knew we were
          splitting. But these were definitely
          mine.

                    FRANK
          Are you and Walt stealing from Mom?

                    BERNARD
          These were mine, Frank.

A SCREECH as Bernard slams on the breaks just avoiding Ivan
who is crossing the street.

                    IVAN
          Woa!

                    BERNARD
          Watch out! Jesus.

Ivan, dressed up in a blazer with jeans and cowboy boots,
peers in the window.

                    IVAN
          Whoops. Hey Bernard. Walt. Hey,
          brother. How's the backhand?

                    FRANK
               (smiling)
          Good.

                                              (CONTINUED)

                              IVAN
                         (whispers)
                    Two hands. No junkyard now.

Frank shakes his head, in agreement.

                              IVAN (CONT'D)
                    Uh, Bernard, Joan says you have a check
                    for me.

                              BERNARD
                    She said that? No, tennis is hers.

                              IVAN
                    She says it's yours.

                              BERNARD
                    She's wrong. In our separation
                    agreement, it says she handles tennis and
                    winter coats. I do sneakers and camp.

                              IVAN
                    Okay, I'll take it up with her.

Ivan winks at Frank and continues on. Bernard drives.

                              BERNARD
                    Ivan's a bit of a half-wit, isn't he?

Walt laughs. So then does Bernard. Frank, annoyed, turns
around to see Ivan climbing the stairs at Joan's.

The car turns the corner, we PAN to a subway stop and down
the stairs.

35   INT/EXT. SUBWAY STATIONS - DAY   35

As the train passes by we see each subway stop on the way to
Bernard's: Parkside, Prospect, Church, Beverly, Cortelyou.
We PAN from the outside of Cortelyou to Bernard's Peugeot as
it pulls up to:

36   EXT. BERNARD'S NEW HOME - DAY   36

His house is a Victorian structure, but pretty dilapidated.
The porch bows to one side, the stairs are rotting. Walt and
Frank climb out of the car, a bit taken aback by this place.
Frank still has the cat. Bernard grins.

37   INT. BERNARD'S NEW HOME - DAY   37

Bernard unlocks the door and he, Walt and Frank enter. It's
quite ramshackled, falling apart. Mismatched, ratty
furniture. Frank puts the cat down.

                    BERNARD
          It was important to me to have a place
          like your mother's. I'm gonna cook and
          run the household like you're used to.

                    FRANK
          This is nothing like our house.

                    BERNARD
          You mean your mother's house.

                    FRANK
          What?

                    BERNARD
          This is nothing like your mother's house.

                    FRANK
          That's what I just said.

                    BERNARD
          No, you said, "our" house. That's your
          mother's house. This is your house too.

                    FRANK
          No, this is your house.

                    BERNARD
          It's our house.

Frank turns to see the cat pissing in the corner.

38   INT. FRANK'S NEW ROOM - DAY   38

The room is already sparsely and randomly decorated, a few
odd posters on the walls. Frank looks at an image of Ilie
Nastase. He shakes his head.

                    FRANK
          I hate Nastase, you know that. Ivan met
          Nastase and said he was an asshole.

                    BERNARD
          Well, I couldn't find Vitas Gerulitis.

                                        (CONTINUED)

                              FRANK
            I have a Vitas poster at home...at Mom's.
            And all my turtles.

                              BERNARD
            We can get you some turtles. I know you
            like the amphibians.

                              FRANK
            Turtles are reptiles.

                              BERNARD
            Here's a desk for you to do your
            homework.

Bernard indicates one of those chair/desks where the writing
slab is attached to the arm of the chair. Frank goes over
and sits in it. He looks horribly uncomfortable.

                              FRANK
            Dad, this is for a lefty.

Bernard says nothing.

39   INT. WALT'S NEW ROOM - NIGHT   39

The Knicks game is coming from the TV downstairs. The room
has been set up with much more care, a few selected books on
a desk and posters of Samuel Beckett and Antonioni's "Blow
Up" tacked to the wall. Walt and Frank each wear one brown
boxing glove. They jab at each other softly.

                              FRANK
            Dad got me a lefty desk.

                              WALT
            Frank, don't be difficult. We need to be
            supportive of Dad.

                              FRANK
            I hate it here.

                              WALT
            Don't be a chick. You can get a righty
            desk later.

                              FRANK
            Why do I want a desk at home anyway? I
            don't want a chalkboard or a bell going
            off every forty-five minutes either.

                                                      (CONTINUED)

                         WALT
               He likes being with us.

                         FRANK
               He likes having us in the house. You got
               books. I didn't get books.

                         WALT
               Cause these are books Dad knows I like.

                         FRANK
               I wanna go back to Mom's.

                         WALT
               Why do you wanna go to Mom's? She caused
               this, chick.

                         FRANK
               No she didn't.

Frank hits Walt with his bare hand.

                         WALT
               Ow, you can't do that.

                         FRANK
               I'm not a chick.

                         WALT
               Yes, you are.
                    (raising his voice)
               And you don't know what you're talking
               about, chick. This is Mom's doing.

                         FRANK
               Stop calling me chick.

                         WALT
               Didn't Mom tell us they would never get
               divorced?

                         FRANK
               Yeah.

                         WALT
               So, Mom's a liar.

Frank hits Walt again with his bare hand, clipping his
brother's ear.

                                          (CONTINUED)

39   CONTINUED: (2)   39

                              WALT (CONT'D)
                    Ow, fuck, that hurt.

Walt punches Frank harder with his glove.

                              FRANK
                    Ow!

Frank wildly smacks Walt with both hands. Walt takes off his
glove, grabs Frank, and pins him to the floor. His knee
digging into Frank's chest.

                              FRANK (CONT'D)
                    I'm not being a chick you fucking ass
                    man!

Walt digs deeper. Frank grimaces in pain.

                              FRANK (CONT'D)
                    You're hurting me. Really hurting me.

Walt's face suddenly grows emotional, he's on the edge of
crying. He releases Frank and sits up. Frank coughs.

                              FRANK (CONT'D)
                    One turtle would've made a difference.

Walt doesn't know how to react. Frank, uneasily, walks out
of the room.

40   INT. FRANK'S ROOM - CONTINUOUS   40

Frank enters, holding his sore chest. He sits in his lefty
desk chair. He buries his head in his arms, but has trouble
since the desk board is on the wrong side.

41   OMITTED   41

42   INT. BERNARD'S COLLEGE OFFICE - DAY   42

The students file out. Lili walks up to Bernard who is
packing up his briefcase, she hands him a story. Walt waits
for his Dad.

                              LILI
                    I hope you like it. Your notes were
                    awesome, Bernard. I loved your idea for
                    the change in tense at the end.

42   CONTINUED: 42

                        BERNARD
            Yeah, I think it could be the coup of the
            story.

                        LILI
            I reread A Hunger Artist on your
            suggestion and stole a couple things.
            See if you can spot them.

                        BERNARD
            Good story to steal from.

She grins at Walt who instantly blushes. She walks away.
They stare at her silently the entire length of the hallway.

43   INT. TENNIS COURTS - DAY   43

Frank hits long. Ivan at the net.

                        FRANK
            Fuck!

                        IVAN
            Frank!

                        FRANK
            Sorry.

Bernard and Walt watch the lesson from the sidelines.

                        WALT
            How long were you and Mom not getting
            along?

                        BERNARD
            Oh...a couple of years.

                        WALT
            Why didn't you tell me?

                        BERNARD
            I thought we would work it out. I wanted
            to. I tried, as you know, I tried very
            hard. Your mother ultimately wasn't
            interested in that.

                        WALT
            Why not?

                                                        (CONTINUED)

                    BERNARD
I think it has very little to do with me.
She could never make up her mind. She'd
pull away and then get angry at me for
not being more aggressive. Her affair
with that man Richard really made it
difficult finally for me to save the
marriage. It became a fait accompli.

Walt's face whitens.

                    WALT
Affair?

Frank makes another error.

                    FRANK
Mother shit fucker!

                    IVAN
Frank!

                    BERNARD
With Richard.

                    WALT
Who's Richard?

                    BERNARD
Oh...man from the neighborhood. I think
she met him at one of Frank's little league
games. A shrink. Seems sort of like an
ordinary guy. Not an intellectual.

                    WALT
How long was she having the affair?

                    BERNARD
Oh...about four years.

                    WALT
You're kidding.

                    BERNARD
No. I thought you knew this.

                    WALT
Umm...no.

Frank double faults.

43   CONTINUED: (2)   43

> FRANK
> Fuck that cock shit!!

> IVAN
> Frank! Relax, brother.

44   INT. JOAN'S LIVING ROOM - DUSK   44

Everything is out of place. The couch and two easy chairs
have been moved part of the way across the room. Joan,
sweating, tries to lift a coffee table from near the
bookshelf over to the window. She gets it a few feet, but
her arms start to shake and she has to let it down. Walt and
Frank enter. Frank dragging his racquet.

> JOAN
> Hey honeys!

> FRANK
> Hey Mom. What are you doing?

> JOAN
> I'm changing things around a bit.

She catches her breath. Walt stops in front of her.

> WALT
> I've come by to tell you I'm not staying
> here anymore.

> JOAN
> Why?

> WALT
> You know why.

> JOAN
> No, I don't.

> WALT
> Frank, do you know why?

> FRANK
> No.

> JOAN
> Why don't you tell me, Walt.

> WALT
> Because you cheated on Dad.

(CONTINUED)

Joan takes a breath. Frank looks at Walt, surprised.

                    JOAN
          How did you hear that?
               (pause)
          Your father told you?

                    WALT
          Yeah, he told me. Why did you, Mom?

                    JOAN
          I...I was having a hard time.

                    WALT
          Where were we during all this? Did you
          bring men home?

Joan pauses, thinking about how to answer.

                    JOAN
          Not while...not...not when your father
          was in town. You guys actually met
          Richard, both of you boys, he came for
          take-out once. You remember? Your
          father was in Seattle. You talked about
          the Stones.

                    WALT
          He had the Sticky Fingers with the real
          zipper?

                    JOAN
               (pause)
          Yeah? I don't remember.

                    WALT
          Oh God. Under our noses. Like a
          brothel. Men coming in and out.

                    FRANK
          Walt, shut up.

                    JOAN
          If you want me to explain, I will.

                    WALT
          I don't wanna hear about it.

                    FRANK
          I do.

44   CONTINUED: (2)   44

                        JOAN
            Well, Walt doesn't so I won't say
            anything.

Joan returns to the coffee table and starts to lift it.

                        FRANK
            Walt can leave.

                        WALT
            You disgust me. You weren't even a writer
            until recently. You just bailed on Dad
            cause he's not as successful as he used
            to be and he hasn't gotten the
            recognition he deserves.

Joan drops the table down. She's caught off-guard.

                        JOAN
            You sound like your father.

                        WALT
            Well, I'm glad I sound like him. You
            disgust me.

                        JOAN
            You're being a shit, Walt.

Walt and Frank are both taken aback.

                        WALT
            I'm taking the cat.

Walt tries to grab the cat which hisses at him. Frank stands
between Walt and the animal.

                        FRANK
            You can't have him, it's his night here!

Walt gives Frank a shove, and leaves, slamming the door for
emphasis.

45   INT. BERNARD'S HOUSE - NIGHT   45

Walt and his father sit in front of the TV watching "Three's
Company". The phone rings. Walt picks it up.

46   INT. FRANK'S ROOM - INTERCUT   46

Tangerine Dream's "Love On A Real Train" from Risky Business
plays on the record player. Frank sits on his bed, shirtless,
a beer in his lap. He checks out his muscle in the mirror,
where he's drawn a tattoo with magic marker that reads: Vitas.

                    FRANK
          She also had an affair with some
          therapist.

47   INT. WALT'S ROOM AT DAD'S - INTERCUT   47

Walt takes the phone into his room, sits on the floor.

                    WALT
          I don't want to know.

                    FRANK
          And Otto's father, Don.

                    WALT
               (blanches)
          Otto's father?

                    FRANK
          Yeah. But it's over.

                    WALT
          Otto. Otto doesn't masturbate.

                    FRANK
          She said the affairs have been kind of
          miserable for her. She's dating now, but
          nothing serious.

                    WALT
          She's crazy. She should keep her affairs
          to herself. I'm not going back to Mom's.

                    FRANK
          You have to. Joint custody.

                    WALT
          Fuck joint custody.

Frank cracks open the beer. Walt reacts to the noise.

                    WALT (CONT'D)
          Is Mom letting you drink soda?

(CONTINUED)

                        FRANK
          Beer.

                        WALT
          Since when do you drink beer?

                        FRANK
          Since recently.

Frank poses in his mirror as if he's hitting a shirtless two
handed backhand.

                        FRANK (CONT'D)
          You think Don and she did it?

                        WALT
          Oh, God, I don't wanna think about it.

                        FRANK
          Imagine Don's dick in Mom's mouth.

                        WALT
               (shocked)
          Who are you? Stop it.

                        FRANK
          I'm just asking. Do you think they do
          that? You think she gets anal sex from
          Don?

                        WALT
               (sadly)
          Stop, okay. It's disgusting. Don't.

Silence on both ends.

48   INT. JOAN'S BATHROOM - NIGHT   48

Frank drinks mouthwash and swallows it. He and Joan look in
the mirror.

                        FRANK
               (touching her face)
          We have the same bone structure.

                        JOAN
          No, you have your Dad's features.

                        FRANK
          Really? Fuck it.

                              JOAN
                         (sternly)
                    Frank...

                              FRANK
                    I thought I had your bone structure.

                              JOAN
                         (matter of factly)
                    No.

They continue to stare in the mirror.

                              FRANK
                    You're ugly.

                              JOAN
                         (hesitates)
                    No, I'm not...pickle. Why would you say
                    that?

                              FRANK
                    Cause I think it's true. I think Carl
                    thinks you're ugly.

                              JOAN
                    I'm not though, sweety--

Joan starts to cry. Frank is startled by this. He suddenly
feels terrible.

                              FRANK
                    I'm sorry, mom. Mom, I'm sorry. I was
                    talking about myself.

Frank takes her hand. Joan starts crying harder.

                              JOAN
                    It's okay. It's okay to say that. You
                    can think I'm ugly if you want.

                              FRANK
                    But I was talking about myself, Mom. I
                    was.

He reaches his arms around her shaking body.

49   INT. JUNIOR HIGHSCHOOL LIBRARY - DAY   49

Frank sits at a table, a book about Arthur Ashe in front of
him. He looks at a GIRL talking to her friend a few tables
away. He gathers his stuff and rises.

We FOLLOW Frank into the stacks to a hidden place in back.
He removes a torn out piece of some porn mag from his bag.
It barely shows anything. He looks around and starts humping
the side of the bookcase. When he's through he reaches into
his pants, takes his semen and spreads it across some books
on the shelf.

50   INT. HIGHSCHOOL CAFETERIA - DAY   50

Walt sits across from Otto. Otto stands, to bus his tray.

                    WALT
          I found out something last night.

                    OTTO
          What's that?

                    WALT
          That your Dad was fucking my mom.

Otto sits.

                    OTTO
          What?

                    WALT
          You heard me.

                    OTTO
          I don't believe it.

Lance and Jeffrey pass. Lance mouths "loser detector" to
Otto. Otto makes a face.

                    WALT
          Yeah, supposedly going on for a year or
          so about two years ago.

Otto shuts his eyes for a moment, letting it sink in.

                    OTTO
          Where'd they do it, you think?

                                        (CONTINUED)

50   CONTINUED: 50

                         WALT
          I don't know. Hotel?

                         OTTO
          What a cliche. Your mom told you this?

                         WALT
          She told Frank who told me.

                         OTTO
          She told Frank? Ugh. I'm so horrified
          by this.

                         WALT
          Thanks.

                         OTTO
          I don't mean by your Mom. She's very
          attractive.

                         WALT
          Thanks.

                         OTTO
          It's just...I guess...do I bring it up at
          dinner tonight?

                         WALT
          It was just an affair. A fuck. We're not
          gonna be brothers or anything. She said
          your Dad's pretty fucked up with women.

                         OTTO
                    (annoyed)
          Well, why did she sleep with him then?

                         WALT
          I don't know. Because she's an asshole.

51   INT. SOPHIE'S PARENTS' LIVING ROOM - DAY   51

      Sophie and Walt drink wine coolers and listen to records.

                         SOPHIE
          Oh, I read The Metamorphosis. You were
          right, it's great.

                         WALT
          Oh?

                                                        (CONTINUED)

                         SOPHIE
          Yeah, I mean so bizarre. What do you
          think is happening at the end with the
          sister?

                         WALT
          Oh...I think she's...it's ambiguous
          really.

                         SOPHIE
          Yeah. I mean, it's gross when he turns
          into the bug, but I love how matter of
          fact everything is.

                         WALT
          Yeah, it's very Kafkaesque.

She looks at him oddly. She laughs.

                         SOPHIE
          Cause it's written by Franz Kakfa.

                         WALT
               (pause)
          Right. I mean, clearly.

She and he meet eyes. He leans in part way, stops. She
follows through and they kiss. His mouth opens, hers doesn't.
They stop for a second, smile at one another and start
kissing again.

                         SOPHIE
          You're shoving the whole tongue in me.

                         WALT
          Oh...sorry.

                         SOPHIE
          S'okay. Just do it a little. Like
          little licks.

                         WALT
               (with his tongue in her mouth)
          Like this?

                         SOPHIE
               (with his tongue in her mouth)
          Yeah.

They kiss for a bit. They release and look at each other.

51   CONTINUED: (2)   51

                         WALT
              I wish you didn't have so many freckles
              on your face.

Sophie is on the edge of a reaction.

                         WALT (CONT'D)
              Not really though. I don't know.

52   INT. BERNARD'S LIVING ROOM - DAY   52

Bernard is opening a letter. It's a form <u>rejection letter</u>
<u>from an agency</u> addressed to Mr. Beckman. He tosses it on the
coffee table, pissed. Frank walks into the room.

                         FRANK
              I'm feeling kind of feverish. Do we have
              any Tylenol?

                         BERNARD
                    (distracted)
              I don't know.

                         FRANK
              I didn't see any.

                         BERNARD
              Then there isn't any.

                         FRANK
              Can we get some?

Bernard goes into his wallet and hands him two dollars.

                         FRANK (CONT'D)
              Is this enough?

                         BERNARD
              Get a small one.

53   INT. DRUGSTORE - DAY   53

Frank puts the Tylenol on the counter. The SALESMAN rings it
up.

                         SALESMAN
              Three fifty-seven.

Frank looks at him, "Really"? The guy waits.

54   EXT. BERNARD'S HOUSE - DAY   54

Bernard, holding the front door open, looks down at Frank.

                BERNARD
        For a small one?

Frank nods. Bernard goes into his pockets, gives Frank two
dollars. Frank, now sweating with fever, turns back around.

55   EXT. BROOKLYN STREET - DAY   55

Frank shuffles out of the store, the Tylenol in his hand. He
looks terrible.

56   INT. BERNARD'S KITCHEN - DAY   56

Frank enters. Bernard is reading the paper.

                FRANK
        I got it.

                BERNARD
        You have change?

Frank digs into his pockets and hands his father back the
forty-three cents.

                BERNARD (CONT'D)
        You wanna play ping pong?

                FRANK
        I'm gonna lie down.

                BERNARD
        One game.

57   INT. BERNARD'S ATTIC - DAY   57

Frank serves it off the table.

                FRANK
        Fuckin' shit!

He slams his paddle on the table.

                BERNARD
        19 to 7. Have you given more thought to
        what you're interested in?

(CONTINUED)

57   CONTINUED:

Frank intentionally hits it out.

> BERNARD (CONT'D)
> Come on, you have to try. It's no fun
> for me if you don't try.

> FRANK
> I want to be a tennis pro like Ivan.

> BERNARD
> Come on, you don't want to be a tennis
> pro.

> FRANK
> Why not?

> BERNARD
> It's not serious. I mean, McEnroe or
> Borg is an artist, it's like dance.
> Connors has a brutish brilliance. But at
> Ivan's level...Ivan is fine, but he's not
> a serious guy. He's a philistine.

> FRANK
> What's a philistine?

> BERNARD
> A guy who doesn't care about books or
> interesting films or things. Your
> mother's brother Ned is also a
> philistine.

> FRANK
> Then I'm a philistine.

> BERNARD
> No, you're interested in books and things.
> You liked The Wild Child when we saw it.

> FRANK
> But lots of people can like that movie.
>   (considering it)
> No, I'm a philistine.

Frank serves. Bernard puts it away.

58   INT. BERNARD'S DINING ROOM/KITCHEN - NIGHT   58

Walt and Frank wait at the dining room table, plates in front
of them with raw carrots, as Bernard, around the corner in
the kitchen, fries up the veal cutlets.

                    BERNARD (O.S)
          When am I going to meet the famous
          Sophie?

                    WALT
          I don't know. She's not gorgeous, but
          she's cute.

                    BERNARD (O.S.)
          You have plenty of time to sleep with
          gorgeous women.

Walt smiles at this thought.

                    BERNARD (O.S.) (CONT'D)
          Goddamn it!

Frank gets up, walks around the corner and peers in the
kitchen. The veal cutlets are scattered on the floor.
Bernard is picking them up, his back to Frank. Frank returns
to the table and Walt.

                    FRANK
          They fell on the floor.

59   MOMENTS LATER   59

Bernard, Walt and Frank sit at the table eating the cutlets.
Frank removes something from his mouth with disgust.

                    BERNARD
          When my first novel came out, I had a lot
          of opportunities. I was with your mother
          so I didn't partake. And I've never had
          an affair with a student, although many
          have come on to me. That's why you might
          not want to be attached at your age. But
          it sounds like Sophie's good for now.

                    FRANK
          Why'd you yell goddamn it?

                                          (CONTINUED)

                         BERNARD
                    (not looking up)
               I burned myself.

                         WALT
               The cutlets are great. Dad, did you hear
               from that agent?

                         BERNARD
               Umm, not yet.

                         WALT
               But if he likes your novel, then you get
               it published, right?

                         BERNARD
               Basically.

                         FRANK
               What happened to your old agent, Fred?

                         BERNARD
               He pissed me off. Made a disparaging
               remark about the Knicks at a party. Said
               they played like thugs. I found it
               really offensive. He's kind of a jerk.

Frank looks down, the bit of porn mag he had before is
between his legs on the chair.

                         BERNARD (CONT'D)
               I think it was important to your mother
               that I achieve some sort of commercial
               success. And when I didn't meet her
               expectations in that area...

He clears his throat. He looks at Walt and shrugs.

60   INT. MIDWOOD HALLWAY - DAY   60

Walt and Sophie pass each other, handing off folded notes.

61   INT. CLASSROOM - MOMENTS LATER   61

Walt takes his seat and opens the loose-leaf note. The
lyrics to Bryan Adams' "Run To You".

62   INT. HIGHSCHOOL PHYSICS LAB - SAME   62

Sophie quickly opens her note too. A typed quote from Sartre
to Simone de Beauvoir.

63   EXT. MIDWOOD HIGH SCHOOL - DAY   63

Walt and Sophie walk together, holding hands.

                    SOPHIE
          What you're going to witness is a
          Greenberg family tradition. Friday night
          Chinese at Hunan Palace. I hope you're
          prepared.

They pass by WENDY CHEN, a classmate. Walt drops Sophie's
hand. They both say, Hi as she passes.

                    SOPHIE (CONT'D)
          Why'd you let go of my hand?

                    WALT
          What?

                    SOPHIE
          When we passed Wendy, you let go.

                    WALT
          I didn't realize.

He picks her hand back up.

64   INT. HUNAN PALACE - DUSK   64

MR. and MRS. GREENBERG, Sophie and Walt. The Waiter brings
them sizzling soup.

                    MRS. GREENBERG
          Walt, is there anything special you'd
          like to order?

                    WALT
          No, I'm just happy to have the same
          amount of dishes as people. In my
          family, it's always one dish less the
          number of people. That's our family
          tradition, not ordering enough food.

(CONTINUED)

64   CONTINUED:

                    MRS. GREENBERG
                        (laughing)
            That's funny. Oh, he's funny, Sophie.

                    SOPHIE
            I know.

Sophie kicks Walt under the table. He looks around at the
family, together, happy. It's all very comfortable.

65   EXT. JOAN'S HOUSE - DUSK   65

Bernard sits in the car. A moment. He gets out, opens the
backseat, takes out the pet carrier. The cat mews from
inside as he walks up the familiar stoop of his old house.
Rings. A beat. Joan opens the front door.

                    JOAN
            You're early.

                    BERNARD
            Hi, Joan.

He hands her the cat.

                    JOAN
            Don't feed him the generic stuff.

                    BERNARD
            What?

                    JOAN
            Frank says you're feeding the cat generic
            food. Get Purina, it's what he likes.

                    BERNARD
            It's the same damn thing, Joan.

                    JOAN
            Okay. It's not, but...

                    BERNARD
            He's my cat too. You remember when he
            got stuck in the wall in New Hampshire
            and I rescued him. I know how to handle
            it.

                    JOAN
            It was a radiator.

                                            (CONTINUED)

                              BERNARD
                    What?

                              JOAN
                    He was stuck in a radiator.

          Bernard says nothing.

                              JOAN (CONT'D)
                    You trimmed your beard.

                              BERNARD
                    It was starting to get a little feral.
                    You look well.

                              JOAN
                    Yeah? Thanks.

                              BERNARD
                    Things are good here. Teaching's going
                    well. And I'm playing the best tennis of
                    my life. Maybe that's an illusion, but it
                    feels that way.

                              JOAN
                        (smiles)
                    That's good.

          Bernard cranes his neck slightly, trying to see over her
          shoulder and into the house.

                              JOAN (CONT'D)
                    Hey, I was thinking we should sit
                    together at Walt's performance next
                    month.

                              BERNARD
                        (pause)
                    Okay.

                              JOAN
                    I think it'd be nice for him if we're
                    both there together. Maybe we could all
                    go out afterwards.

                              BERNARD
                    Mmm. I don't know. Maybe. Okay, maybe.
                    I think he's getting quite good at
                    guitar.

                         JOAN
          I know. The stuff he's writing is really
          wonderful. Have you met his girlfriend?

                         BERNARD
          No. He talks about her with me, though.

                         JOAN
          Good. I'd appreciate it if you didn't
          tell him about things like Richard...

Silence.

                         BERNARD
          My father told me you called him.

                         JOAN
               (pause)
          I did, yeah.

                         BERNARD
          He said you...he said you were upset.

                         JOAN
          Yeah. I wanted to...I like him. You
          know that. I just wanted to say...I
          don't know. I wanted to say, Hello.

                         BERNARD
          He called me right after. He said,
          "Bernie, I think you can save your
          marriage."

Joan, uncomfortable, says nothing.

                         BERNARD (CONT'D)
          I told him I didn't think there was
          anything else I could do. I did try
          everything.

Tears start to spill down Joan's face. A pause and Bernard
turns and walks toward the car.

                         JOAN
          Bye Bernard.

She shuts the door.

66   INT. BERNARD'S CLASSROOM - DAY   66

    Lili approaches Bernard as he's packing up. Walt waits.

                         LILI
              Bernard, I was wondering if you knew of
              any apartments. I'm being kicked out of
              my sub-let. Unless I, I don't know, blow
              the super, I'm out on my ass.

                         BERNARD
              Oh...I don't...

                         LILI
                    (to Walt)
              I guess you don't know either, huh?

                         WALT
                    (glad to be asked)
              Oh...nope.

                         BERNARD
              Actually, I have an extra room in my
              house. You could stay there till you
              find something.
                    (pause)
              And you wouldn't have to blow your super.

    Walt's eyes widen. Lili smiles wryly.

                         LILI
              Oh wow, I guess...I'd hate to put you
              out.

                         BERNARD
              No, no.

                         LILI
              Or your kids.

                         WALT
              No, no.

67   INT. BERNARD'S FOYER - DAY   67

    Bernard helps Lili carry her bags in. Walt, trails, his eyes
    on Lili's ass, packed into her tight jeans.

68   INT. GUEST ROOM - DAY   68

Lili enters. The "Blow Up" poster is now on her wall. She
turns around. Bernard and Walt stand in the doorway, smiles
plastered on their faces.

                    LILI
          Blow Up. Looks like a cool movie.

                    WALT
          It's a classic. I had it in my room.

                    BERNARD
          The bathroom is right across the hall.
          You'll have to share with the kids, but
          they can come upstairs and use mine.

                    LILI
          I don't care. As long as Walt remembers
          to put the seat down. Thank you,
          Bernard. Thank you, Walt.

Bernard and Walt just keep grinning.

69   INT. BERNARD'S ATTIC - NIGHT   69

Bernard plays ping pong with Frank.

                    BERNARD
          Joan told me you don't like your sheets.

                    FRANK
          They're fine.

                    BERNARD
          And that you disapprove of the food I
          feed the cat. You should tell me these
          things, not her.

Bernard serves the ball off the table.

                    BERNARD (CONT'D)
          FUCK!!

                    FRANK
          15! 15/20.

He serves, they rally, both their faces tense. Frank wins
again. Bernard slams his racquet onto the table.

                                                    (CONTINUED)

69   CONTINUED: 69

                         BERNARD
          Motherfucker! I can't believe this!

                         FRANK
          My serve.

     Frank quick-serves Bernard who hits it out.

                         BERNARD
          I wasn't ready.

                         FRANK
          Yes, you were.

                         BERNARD
               (stern)
          Frank, I was not ready.

70   INT. KITCHEN - SAME   70

     Lili, dressed to go out, looks in the fridge. Walt watches
     her. We can hear the ping pong from upstairs.

                         LILI
          This is Mother Hubbard. There's nothing
          to eat or drink. No soda.

                         WALT
          We're not allowed soda.

                         LILI
          I guess there's two kinds of parents,
          those who allow soda and sugar cereal and
          those who don't.

     We hear a "I can't believe this shit!" from the attic. Lili
     wipes her hands with a paper towel and tosses it in the
     garbage.

                         WALT
          We're not supposed to use paper towels to
          wipe our hands. The cloth is for that.

                         LILI
          You're cute.

                         WALT
          Thanks.

                                               (CONTINUED)

70   CONTINUED: 70

          She touches his head, a kind of a gentle caress, and
          disappears into the other room. Walt goes into the garbage
          and finds the paper towel. He stuffs it in his pocket.

71   INT. BERNARD'S ATTIC - SAME   71

          They rally. Tensions flaring. Bernard hits what looks like
          a winner, Frank dives and returns it. Bernard hits another
          shot which Frank lunges and gets back. A looper which
          Bernard slams for a winner. Frank, staggers back, hitting
          his head on the wall.

                         FRANK
              Shit!!

          Bernard instantly eases up, now that he's won.

                         BERNARD
              Good game. It's hard to beat your
              father.

          Frank chucks his paddle across the table, just missing
          Bernard and thudding into the wall.

                         BERNARD (CONT'D)
              Hey! Watch out.

          Frank walks past his Dad and down the stairs.

                         FRANK
                    (under his breath)
              Suck my dick, ass man.

72   INT. BERNARD'S LIVING ROOM - NIGHT   72

          Bernard watches Lili, through the window, on the front porch.
          She's greeted by the burly, curly haired man from Bernard's
          class. They disappear out of his sight. Bernard looks
          annoyed and disappointed. A light clicks on. Walt walks by,
          his coat on.

                         BERNARD
              Where you going?

                         WALT
              The movies. And then to a party. With
              Sophie. What are you going to do?

                                                        (CONTINUED)

                              BERNARD
                    Umm, I don't know. Frank won't leave his
                    room. He's being difficult.

Walt looks at his Dad. He looks sad, vulnerable.

                              WALT
                    You wanna come to the movie?

                              BERNARD
                    Okay. Not the party, but the movie.

                              WALT
                    We were thinking "Short Circuit".

                              BERNARD
                    "Blue Velvet" is supposed to be quite
                    interesting.

73   OMITTED   73

74   INT. MOVIE THEATER - NIGHT   74

On screen, a naked and bruised Isabella Rossellini steps out
on to her porch. Walt and Bernard, with Sophie between them,
watch. Sophie glances over at Bernard for a second, then
back to the movie. She looks horribly embarrassed.

75   INT. FRANK'S NEW ROOM - NIGHT   75

Frank, shirtless, a beer on his lefty desk, inspects himself
in the mirror. He talks to his reflection in a loud whisper,
acting out some imaginary scenario.

                              FRANK
                    No!...Stop!...Frank, No!...

He stops, looks around and starts packing his knapsack.

76   INT. DINER - NIGHT   76

Bernard, Walt and Sophie in a booth, eating burgers.

                              BERNARD
                    A student of mine writes very racy short
                    stories you might like.

                              SOPHIE
                    Oh?

                                                        (CONTINUED)

76   CONTINUED:

                    BERNARD
          Yeah, she has one that chronicles her
          vagina.

                    WALT
               (blushing)
          Dad...

                    SOPHIE
          Oh, that...that sounds interesting.

                    BERNARD
          Very feminist, but very interesting.

                    SOPHIE
          Uh huh.

Silence. The Waitress brings the check. Bernard goes for
his wallet. Sophie, politely takes out a few bills and hands
them to Bernard. He takes her money. Walt watches this
interaction, embarrassed.

77   INT. BERNARD'S HOUSE - NIGHT   77

Bernard enters alone.

                    BERNARD
          Frank, I'm back!

He walks upstairs and down the hall.

                    BERNARD (CONT'D)
          Frank?

He looks into Frank's room. It's empty. He looks in the
bathroom, his room, Walt's room. He jogs down the stairs.

                    BERNARD (CONT'D)
          Frank!

78   INT/EXT. BERNARD'S PEUGEOT - NIGHT   78

Bernard drives through his neighborhood, scanning the street.
He turns a corner. Frank, his knapsack on, lugging a duffle,
is walking at a brisk pace toward the subway. Bernard speeds
up and pulls along side of him. Frank turns, his face
dropping when he sees his Dad.

79   MOMENTS LATER   79

Bernard drives. Frank next to him, quietly steaming.

                    BERNARD
          What were you doing?

                    FRANK
          I was going to Mom's.

                    BERNARD
          You don't do that on my night. Ever.
          You hear me?

                    FRANK
          Yes.

                    BERNARD
          I'm your father, you listen to what I
          say.

                    FRANK
          But you were out.

                    BERNARD
          It's still my night, dammit!

                    FRANK
          Okay, okay.

Bernard turns the corner, looks to park.

                    BERNARD
          Shit, and someone got my space.
          Goddammit! Son. Of. A. Bitch.

                    FRANK
          Sorry.

Bernard stops at a light. A moment. Frank unbuckles, and is
out the door. Running.

                    BERNARD
          Frank!

80   INT. MOM'S LIVING ROOM - NIGHT   80

Frank enters, the room is dim. A record plays on the stereo.
The furniture has now been successfully rearranged.

(CONTINUED)

80   CONTINUED:

                         FRANK
                  Hello! Hello!!

The sounds of footsteps. Joan, in a man's oxford shirt and
underwear, comes down the steps.

                         JOAN
                  Frank? What are you doing here? It's
                  not your night with me.

                         FRANK
                  I don't wanna look like Dad.

                         JOAN
                  Looks aren't everything. It's not your
                  night with me, Sweetie.

Frank notices an empty bottle of champagne on the coffee table.

                         FRANK
                  Did you have a party?

                         JOAN
                  I celebrated. Knopf is publishing my
                  novel. Pickle, you should be at your
                  Dad's.

                         FRANK
                  Yeah?

                         JOAN
                  Yeah. I need some nights without you
                  guys sometimes.

Frank nods, disappointed. His eyes settle on a second glass
and plate. He looks up at his Mom.

                         JOAN (CONT'D)
                  I...someone's here.

Heavier footsteps sound and a sheepish looking Ivan comes
down the stairs in a t-shirt and jeans. Frank just stares.

                         IVAN
                  What's up, brother?

                         FRANK
                  Nothing.

81   INT. LANCE'S PARENTS' LIVING ROOM - NIGHT   81

Walt and Sophie, Lance and Lara, Jeffrey and Susan mingle
like they're adults. Otto is alone. Everyone smokes.

                    LANCE
          Jeffrey, what can I getcha?

                    JEFFREY
               (suave)
          Gin fizz. Bond's drink. Sophie?

                    SOPHIE
          Umm, rum and tonic.

                    LANCE
               (smooth)
          A rum and tonic lady. And a Bartles and
          James and Coke for me.

The phone rings. Lance picks it up.

                    LANCE (CONT'D)
          Hello?

He hands the receiver to Walt. Walt looks to Sophie, "Weird".

82   INT/EXT. BERNARD'S PEUGEOT - NIGHT   82

Bernard drives. Walt next to him, a little buzzed.

                    BERNARD
          He just took off and went to your
          mother's. It's my night, he knows that.

                    WALT
          Do you ever think we could ease up on
          whose night is whose?

                    BERNARD
          I wanna see you guys. I love you.

Silence.

                    WALT
          Did you like Sophie?

                    BERNARD
          Yeah. I think she's fine. Is she a
          Knicks fan?

                                              (CONTINUED)

> WALT
> I don't know. You think she's pretty?

> BERNARD
> Sure, but she's not the type I go for.
> You just have to decide if you want to be
> attached. It's good to play the field at
> your age.

> WALT
> (offhand)
> Lili is pretty.

They pull up in front of Joan's place.

> BERNARD
> Mmm. Would you go ring the bell. I hate
> walking up those steps. It's very
> uncomfortable for me. Very painful. I
> used to live in this house.
> (off Walt's look)
> As you know.

Walt nods and climbs out of the car.

83   INT. BATHROOM - NIGHT   83

Joan opens the bathroom door. The shower is running.

> JOAN
> Pickle, your Dad and Walt are here and
> they're going to take you back to
> Bernard's.

Frank casually responds from the other side of the curtain.

> FRANK
> I'll be right out.

> JOAN
> I'm sorry about...about you seeing Ivan
> like this. I would've liked to have told
> you before you saw him.

84   EXT. JOAN'S HOUSE - NIGHT   84

From Frank's window, Joan watches her sons walk to Bernard's
idling car. Walt and she meet eyes. He turns away and climbs
in the car. Frank suddenly stops at the curb and doesn't get
in. He stands there. Everyone waits. CUT TO BLACK.

85   INT. WALT'S ROOM AT DAD'S - NIGHT   85

Walt, his homework spread on the floor, sings along to the
lyrics of a record. Bernard enters holding the phone.

                    BERNARD
          Your mother.

Walt hesitates. Bernard indicates that he should take it.

                    WALT
               (pause)
          Hello.

86   INT. JOAN'S ROOM - INTERCUT   86

Joan sits on the side of her bed, a glass of sherry on the end
table. Her hand shakes slightly. She takes a deep breath.

                    JOAN
          Hi.
               (trying to get it all out)
          I wanted to tell you about Ivan so you
          didn't hear it from anyone else.
               (pause)
          Frank may've already said something.

                    WALT
          He did.

                    JOAN
          I've been seeing him a short time. But I
          like him and I thought you guys should
          know that. And meet him. I mean, I know
          you know him, I mean meet him this way.
          And...do you have any questions?

                    WALT
          No.

                    JOAN
          Umm...there was something else I was
          going to say...Oh, I ran into Celia,
          Lance's mother, on the street and she was
          telling me how wonderful she thinks you
          are. How polite and funny you are...

                    WALT
          Uh huh.

                                              (CONTINUED)

                              JOAN
          She said there was something you did with
          the salt and pepper shakers, a little
          play or something.

                              WALT
          It was kind of stupid.

                              JOAN
          I said, I know all those things about him
          already. But it's nice to hear it.
                    (pause)
          I remember what else I was going to say.
          I wanted to know if you'd be interested
          in coming to dinner on Saturday because
          I'm having the Dicksteins over--

                              WALT
          I'm going to a party on Saturday and I'm
          sleeping at Jeffrey's.

                              JOAN
                    (pause)
          That's okay.

Silence.

                              WALT
          I'm gonna go to bed.

                              JOAN
          Okay. Goodnight, chicken.

                              WALT
          Night.

He hangs up. So does she.

87   INT. HIGHSCHOOL AUDITORIUM - DAY   87

Kids line up as MR. SIMIC, 40's, goes through the order of
performers for the talent show. Walt sits on the edge of the
stage with Lance, Jeffrey and Otto around him. Lance safety
pins his jeans. A young GIRL practices her song.

                              LANCE
          You think she likes you?

                              WALT
          I get a feeling, yeah.

                                                         (CONTINUED)

87   CONTINUED:

                    LANCE
        What about Sophie?

                    WALT
        If I can lose it to Lili, I'll do it. I
        mean, I bet she's great in bed.

                    JEFFREY
        She can probably move her pussy muscles
        just the right way so you blow your load
        in like seconds.

                    WALT
        It'd be pretty great.

                    LANCE
        Maybe do 'em both. Why not?

They all nod in agreement.

                    OTTO
        Oh, I jerked off. You're right. It's
        good.

They all look at Otto.

88   INT. TENNIS COURTS - DUSK   88

Joan and Frank enter. Frank initially won't meet Ivan's eye,
but Ivan smiles warmly.

                    IVAN
        Hey, brother. How's the grip?

                    FRANK
        Fine.
            (pause)
        Do you think you and I are philistines?

                    JOAN
        Frank!

                    IVAN
        What's a philistine?

                    FRANK
        Someone who doesn't like books or
        interesting movies and things.

Bernard enters, taken aback to see Joan with Ivan and Frank.

                                              (CONTINUED)

88   CONTINUED: 88

                         BERNARD
              Oh...you're still here. It's my night
              with him.

                         JOAN
              I know, I thought I'd watch him hit.

They stand in silence. Ivan gives Frank a kind of half
shrug. Frank gives him a half shrug back. Joan walks over
to a bench and takes a seat.

Ivan, Frank and Bernard stand there awkwardly. Bernard turns
to Ivan.

                         BERNARD
              You married?

                         IVAN
              No.

                         BERNARD
              The whole thing's very complicated.

89   INT/EXT. BERNARD'S PEUGEOT - DUSK   89

Bernard starts the car. Frank shotgun, practicing his grip.

                         FRANK
              Mom's dating Ivan.

Bernard turns the ignition off.

                         BERNARD
              Really? Ivan, back there, Ivan?

                         FRANK
              Yeah.

                         BERNARD
              Are you sure? Why didn't you say
              something? Why is your mother dating all
              these jocks? Very uninteresting men.

                         FRANK
              Ivan is very interesting.

                         BERNARD
              Ivan's not a serious possibility for your
              mother.

                                                      (CONTINUED)

89   CONTINUED: 89

                                  FRANK
        I think he is.

                                BERNARD
        I'm telling you he isn't, Frank. You'll
        see. He won't last.

                                  FRANK
        I want him to last.

                                BERNARD
          (thrown)
        Why? You'll get over Ivan. As you get
        older, you'll get more interested in
        writing or arts of some kind. Tennis
        will get less important.
          (clearly upset)
        I don't want to bad mouth Ivan. But I
        don't know what Joan is thinking.

                                  FRANK
        I think Ivan is--

                                BERNARD
        Frank!

Frank glances over at his Dad. Bernard brushes a tear from
his cheek. Frank turns away quickly. The car pulls into
traffic.

90   OMITTED   90

91   INT. SOPHIE'S PARENTS' BEDROOM - NIGHT   91

They both lie on the king size bed, kissing. Sophie has her
hand in his underwear and she moves it up and down.

                                WALT
        Oww!

                                SOPHIE
        Sorry. Was that too hard?

                                WALT
        Yeah, a bit.

She readjusts her technique.

                                SOPHIE
        Is that better?

                     WALT
         Yeah...that's gooo--

Sophie is taken aback as Walt twitches and comes.

                     SOPHIE
         Oh.

                     WALT
          (trying to act cool)
         I guess...I...I don't know what...why
         that happened.

                     SOPHIE
         It's okay. I mean, it's...okay.

She gets up and goes into the bathroom. Walt lies there, for
a moment, feeling exposed, yanks up his pants. Sophie
returns with a towel. She scrubs the wet spot on the
comforter.

                     WALT
         Sorry.

                     SOPHIE
         Don't be sorry.

                     WALT
         I don't know why I didn't last longer, I
         usually go for much longer.

                     SOPHIE
         It's okay. I guess I can take it as a
         compliment.

                     WALT
         Did you take your shirt off for Nelson
         Barton?

                     SOPHIE
          (silence)
         I don't want to talk about it, Walt.

                     WALT
          Please, it's important.

                     SOPHIE
         Why is it important?

(CONTINUED)

91   CONTINUED: (2)

                         WALT
          Cause I need to know what happened.

                         SOPHIE
          Well...he felt me up and I touched him.

                         WALT
          Down his pants?

                         SOPHIE
          Walt... Yeah.

                         WALT
          I just...from what I can tell. Not an
          intellectual.

                         SOPHIE
                  (pause)
          I'm a virgin.

                         WALT
                  (pause)
          So am I.

92   INT. BERNARD'S DINING ROOM - SAME   92

      Bernard and Lili eat veal cutlets.

                         LILI
          When is your next book coming out?

                         BERNARD
          Soon, I hope. Soon.

                         LILI
          Who's publishing it?

                         BERNARD
          Well, I'm looking for a new agent first.

                         LILI
          A friend of mine's an agent with Binky
          Urban. If you like, I'll show it to him.

                         BERNARD
                  (brightening)
          That'd be great.

      The phone rings. Bernard gets up to answer it.

93   INT. SOPHIE'S PARENTS' BEDROOM - INTERCUT   93

Walt sits on the edge of the bed, nervous about this
conversation. Sophie is still scrubbing the comforter.

                    WALT
          Would...would it be okay...could I stay
          the night at Sophie's?

Lili slides by Bernard with the plates.

                    BERNARD
          Thanks for doing that.
               (to Walt)
          Okay, I'll see you tomorrow. Er,
          Tuesday, I'll see you Tuesday.

                    WALT
               (surprised)
          You don't need me home for anything?

                    BERNARD
          No, everything's fine.

94   INT. BERNARD'S KITCHEN - NIGHT   94

Bernard watches Lili do the dishes.

                    BERNARD
          If you're interested, Walt and I are
          taking a road trip to Suny Binghampton in
          a couple of weekends. I'm giving a
          reading and an ex-student of mine, now
          friend, Jeb Gelber, is fete-ing me with a
          dinner.

                    LILI
          Excellent. You should read the cathedral
          scene from Under Water.

                    BERNARD
          I've done that one a lot. I thought I'd
          do something new... But okay, maybe...

They meet eyes for a moment. And then their lips come
together. Lili withdraws and wipes her nose. She laughs,
slightly embarrassed.

                    LILI
          Sorry, my nose is running.

                                              (CONTINUED)

94   CONTINUED: 94

She moves back in, Bernard pauses.

                    BERNARD
          I'm your teacher.

                    LILI
          I've wondered for a long time what it'd
          be like to fuck you.

95   INT. SOPHIE'S PARENTS' BEDROOM - NIGHT   95

Walt's face, anxious, looks up at the ceiling almost as if
he's reacting to Lili's previous remark. They lie on the bed.

                    WALT
          Umm...I think we should wait.

Sophie rolls over on top of Walt.

                    SOPHIE
          Really?

                    WALT
          Yeah, let's wait.

Sophie rolls back over. Silence.

96   INT. JUNIOR HIGHSCHOOL BATHROOM - DAY   96

In a stall, Frank rubs up against the door. As he finishes,
he reaches into his underpants and takes some semen in his
hand.

97   INT. JUNIOR HIGHSCHOOL HALLWAY - DAY   97

Frank walks down the empty hallway. He comes up to a locker
decorated by a girl. A sign reads, "Erica's locker, Keep
Out". Frank very slowly kisses the metal door. Then smears
his semen on the locker. We DISSOLVE TO:

98   INT. HIGHSCHOOL AUDITORIUM - DUSK   98

Packed with students, parents and teachers. Mr. Simic is the
MC. Five TEACHERS sit at a table with a sign that reads
"Judges" on it. They are all in their 60's and 70's. Tony,
whom we met earlier, finishes an elaborate puppet show with
big paper mache animals. Applause. He bows and walks off.

98   CONTINUED: 98

                         MR. SIMIC
                            (reading)
                  Okay, up next, Walt Berkman who is going
                  to play us a song!

Applause. Lance, Otto and Jeffrey goof around in their
seats. Bernard and Lili sit together. A few rows back,
Joan, Frank and Ivan smile with anticipation. Bernard looks
back and watches Joan and Ivan for a beat. Sophie sits with
her friends, she clasps her hands nervously.

                         WALT
                  Thank you. I'm going to plead guitar...
                            (correcting himself)
                  ...play lead guitar and do vocals on a
                  song...I wrote.

His hands are shaking a bit. He starts to play and relax and
sing "Hey You". Frank's smile drops as he realizes what song
Walt's doing. The crowd, both adults and kids, has a mixed
reaction, some recognizing the song, others enjoying it as an
original. Bernard looks proud, Lili with a sly smile. Ivan
furrows his brow, knowing the song. Joan clearly does not.
Sophie beams.

99   TIME CUT   99

A crowd is around Walt who holds a first place check and
certificate. Bernard hugs him. Otto and Jeffrey slap him on
the back, Lance can be heard saying to another STUDENT: "He
could've written it". Sophie gives Walt a shy kiss on the
cheek.

                         SOPHIE
                  That song was so good!

                         WALT
                  Oh, Dad, you remember Sophie.

                         BERNARD
                  Uh huh.

Sophie shakes Bernard's hand. Walt turns to Lili, blushing.

                         WALT
                  And...Lili.

Sophie shakes Lili's hand as well. Lili raises an eyebrow to
Walt regarding Sophie. Walt takes a step away, distancing
himself from Sophie for Lili's benefit.

                                                    (CONTINUED)

                          LILI
How much did you win?

                          WALT
Hundred bucks.

                          LILI
Come by my room tonight before you go to
bed, I want to show you something.

                          WALT
         (intrigued)
Okay.

Joan, Frank and Ivan approach.

                     WALT (CONT'D)
And this is my Mom and Frank and Ivan.

Sophie shakes their hands. Ivan looks at Walt, a knowing
smile.

                          IVAN
Some song, brother.

                          WALT
Thanks.

Bernard gives Ivan a look. Ivan smiles, politely.

                          IVAN
Hi, Bernard.

Bernard grunts and turns away. Walt's attention turns to
Kate Roache a few feet away, who eyes him back. Sophie's
smile fades as she watches this.

100   EXT. MIDWOOD HIGHSCHOOL - NIGHT   100

They all spill out into the street. Joan approaches Walt,
apprehensively. Ivan horses around with Frank.

                          JOAN
I thought we'd all have dinner. Ivan
suggested Gage and Tollner. We could
celebrate my book and your song.

                          WALT
Nah, I'm gonna go with Dad.

>   JOAN
>   Well, your Dad and I talked about all of
>   us going.

>   WALT
>   I don't want to do that.   See ya.

>   JOAN
>   Ivan and I came to see your show, don't
>   treat us that way.

>   WALT
>   (sarcastic)
>   Oh, thanks for coming to see my show.
>   How nice of you.

Joan grabs both of Walt's arms and pulls him toward her.

>   JOAN
>   You think you hate me, but I know you
>   don't.

Walt yanks free and starts to walk away. Over his shoulder,
he flips her the finger. Joan grabs his arm, whips him
around and slaps him across the face.

Frank is startled, but sneaks out a smile. Other students
and parents watch this. Walt looks at her stunned and
humiliated. After a beat, he turns and walks away toward
Bernard and Lili, passing a kid who says to another kid:
"That's a Floyd song".

101   INT. RESTAURANT - NIGHT   101

Bernard, Walt, Sophie and Lili look at their menus.

>   SOPHIE
>   Where did you come up with some of those
>   lyrics?

>   BERNARD
>   They were very dreamlike. Reminds me of
>   my second novel, End of The Line.
>   There's a rock star character in that.

>   LILI
>   I love that novel.

                  WALT
A classic. The scenes with the baby in
the middle are based on me as a baby.

                  BERNARD
That's right. It's Mailer's favorite of
my books.

                  LILI
And I loved your wife's piece in the New
Yorker.

                  BERNARD
Really? In The New Yorker?
        (to Walt)
Did you know about that?

                  WALT
I guess I did.

                  BERNARD
How'd that happen?

                  LILI
It's an excerpt.

                  WALT
She's getting a novel published.

                  BERNARD
Really?

Bernard's face starts to drain of color.

                  SOPHIE
Walt showed it to me. It was kind of
sad, but really good.

Silence at the table. Bernard turns to his menu.

                  BERNARD
The portions are very big here, you only
need a half order.

                  WALT
Okay.

Walt and Lili meet eyes.

102   EXT. PARKING LOT - NIGHT   102

Bernard still looks disturbed as he hands his ticket to the
ATTENDENT. Walt stands with him. Lili and Sophie smoke in
the background, talking.

                    BERNARD
          Jesus, fifteen dollars for parking.

                    WALT
          What do you think I should do about
          Sophie?

                    BERNARD
          You'll make the right decision. I regret
          sometimes I wasn't more of a free agent when I
          was younger. There was a woman who approached
          me at a party at George Plimpton's after my
          first book. She was very sexy. I could've
          gone home with her.

                    WALT
          Why didn't you?

                    BERNARD
          I was with your mother.

                    WALT
          Oh, right, of course. You should've
          probably done it. It didn't stop her.

They both soak in this remark.

                    BERNARD
          Well, maybe you should sleep with her
          once and see if you like it. It doesn't
          mean you can't see other women too.

                    WALT
               (looking over at the girls)
          I don't know if Sophie will go for that.

                    BERNARD
          Well...after your performance tonight,
          things might change for you.

                    WALT
          Don't you think the first girl you sleep
          with should be perfect?

                                              (CONTINUED)

102 CONTINUED:

                         BERNARD
            You've never made love with one of your
            girlfriends?

                         WALT
            No. I've done other things. I've never
            really had many girlfriends. This is the
            first one, really.

103 EXT. BROOKLYN STREET - NIGHT   103

Walt and Sophie walk together.

                         SOPHIE
            Should we go to my house? I thought we
            could--

                         WALT
            Jesus, you really want to do it, don't
            you.

                         SOPHIE
                (embarrassed)
            I don't know.

                         WALT
            What's the obsession with sex?

                         SOPHIE
            It's not an obsession. I'm not so sure I
            want to do it either. I'm scared too.

                         WALT
            Scared is not the issue. It's just that
            everything is so serious suddenly. We're
            not getting married. You're going to
            Italy anyway for the summer and then to
            college. I just...we're young, we
            shouldn't tie each other down.

                         SOPHIE
            What are you saying?

                         WALT
            Nothing, it's just I don't want to feel
            pressure from you.

                         SOPHIE
            Do you like someone else? Your Dad's
            girlfriend?

                                                    (CONTINUED)

103   CONTINUED:

>   WALT
>   No...why...no! And she's not his
>   girlfriend.
>
>   SOPHIE
>   (she holds back tears)
>   My father said you have a weak handshake
>   which is a sign of indecision.
>
>   WALT
>   (defensive)
>   His hands are so huge, I can't get a good
>   grip.
>
>   SOPHIE
>   And my mother said that you don't have a
>   very good model for relationships because
>   of your parents.
>
>   WALT
>   What? Your mother doesn't know anything.
>   (thrown)
>   I thought it went well. You told me she
>   said I was hilarious.

She bursts into tears. Walt stands there, completely
unprepared for her reaction. She just gets worse and worse,
crying harder and harder.

>   WALT (CONT'D)
>   Stop it. Sophie. Stop it. Don't be
>   difficult. Please.

Her crying stops. She looks at Walt. Silence.

>   SOPHIE
>   I'm not being difficult.

104   INT. LILI'S ROOM - NIGHT   104

Walt sits on the bed next to Lili who's in shorts,
crosslegged. He looks depressed.

>   LILI
>   You want a beer?

She rises and grabs two from a little fridge which is stocked
with stuff.

                    LILI (CONT'D)
      I couldn't take relying on your Dad's
      shopping habits anymore. You can have
      anything you want whenever.

                    WALT
      Thanks.

                    LILI
      I'm going to read you a draft of my new
      story. I want your thoughts first. Then
      I'm gonna show it to your Dad.

Lili lights up a cigarette.

                    LILI (CONT'D)
      You like Pink Floyd, huh?

                    WALT
      What?

Walt tenses up, but she smiles warmly, indicating it's okay.

                    LILI
      Don't worry, I used to hand in Lou Reed
      lyrics in my poetry class and pass them
      off as my own. Although I hope you don't
      get caught. I always did.

She touches his arm. He and she lock eyes for a moment.
Walt bows his head, his eyes on her bare thigh. The crease
in her knee. He focuses in on this. The silence seems to go
on forever.

                    LILI (CONT'D)
      Do you--?

Walt nervously swings his head up, clocking her in the nose.

                    LILI (CONT'D)
      Oww! Fuck.

                    WALT
      Sorry!

Her nose is bleeding.

                    WALT (CONT'D)
      Lili, sorry.

                               (CONTINUED)

104 CONTINUED: (2)   104

She gets up and looks in the mirror.

                    LILI
          Shit. S'okay. Just a bloody nose.

                    WALT
          I'm sorry.

She goes into the bathroom. A moment. She comes out, her
head tilted back, tissues soaking up the blood.

                    LILI
          I think I might take a bath. Okay?

                    WALT
          Oh...okay.

A pause. He realizes he's supposed to go.

                    WALT (CONT'D)
          Okay...

                    LILI
          Night.

He leaves the room.

105 INT. HALLWAY - CONTINUOUS   105

Walt shuffles toward his room, his Dad comes up the stairs.
Stops in his tracks.

                    WALT
          Hey.

                    BERNARD
          Hey.

Walt continues into his room and shuts the door. Bernard
goes into Lili's room.

106 EXT. JOAN'S HOUSE - MORNING   106

Joan and Ivan pack up Ivan's car. Frank stands on the stoop.

                    JOAN
          When's Bernard coming to get you?

                    FRANK
          In an hour.

                                              (CONTINUED)

                    JOAN
          Plan on thirty minutes. He's always early
          to get you. And late to bring you back.

                    FRANK
          I wish I could come with you guys.

                    IVAN
          I heard that, brother.

                    JOAN
          I know. But Dad's got you on Saturday.
               (pause)
          Do you like his girlfriend?

                    FRANK
          Is she his girlfriend?

                    JOAN
          I thought so. She lives with you. He
          doesn't say?

                    FRANK
          No. I think Walt loves her.

                    JOAN
          So, they like the same women now too.

                    FRANK
          What?

                    JOAN
          Nothing. You got our number in Maine.
          Remember to lock up.

                    FRANK
          I will.

                    JOAN
          See you next week, Pickle-oo.

                    FRANK
          Just "Pickle" please.

                    JOAN
          See you next week Just Pickle.

They hug. He and Ivan shake hands.

                                              (CONTINUED)

106   CONTINUED: (2)   106

                         IVAN
            Good grip, brother. Just like Vitas.

                         FRANK
            You too, brother.

    Frank watches, anxiously, as they start the car and drive
    away.

107   INT. JOAN'S LIVING ROOM - MORNING   107

    Frank waits at the window, looking out at the street. Checks
    his watch. Goes to the phone and dials. Machine.

                         FRANK
            Dad, it's me. Are you there?

    He waits and hangs up. Goes to the fridge and takes out a beer.

108   EXT. UPSTATE NEW YORK - MORNING   108

    A crisp spring day. Bernard's Peugeot passes by.

109   INT/EXT. BERNARD'S PEUGEOT - MORNING   109

    Bernard drives, Lili shotgun, Walt in back. Spirits are high.

110   EXT. BINGHAMPTON UNIVERSITY - DAY   110

    Bernard, Walt and Lili are welcomed by JEB GELBER, who wears
    a sweater vest and bolo.

111   INT. COLLEGE AUDITORIUM - DUSK   111

    Bernard reads from Under Water at a podium. Not a well
    attended event. Lili and Walt sit next to each other. His
    arm brushes hers on the arm rest.

    Bernard finishes. Applause. He grins. Gelber comes out and
    shakes his hand.

                         GELBER
                    (under his breath)
            Sorry about the turnout, lots of the kids
            go home early for Passover.

                         BERNARD
                    (pleased anyway)
            They seem to like it.

112   INT. JOAN'S BEDROOM - NIGHT   112

Tangerine Dream's El theme from Risky Business plays on the
stereo. Frank, nude, drinking whiskey, stands at his
mother's dresser going through old photos and jewelry. He
finds some condoms. Takes one out of its wrapper, looks at
it, smells it. And puts it on his penis. He walks over to a
mirror and looks at himself. The condom slips off his penis
and lands on the floor. He retrieves it and tries to put it
back on. On the bed, we now see, he's laid out his mother's
underwear and bra and stockings on the comforter.

Leaning in to the mirror, he moves his nose around. Swigs
from his whiskey glass. Suddenly he doesn't feel so great.
He spits on the floor. Waits. He vomits. He runs to the
bathroom.

113   INT. BATHROOM - CONTINUOUS   113

He throws up into the toilet. Tears stream down his face.
He rolls over onto the tile. A moment. He sneezes. He
looks into his hand and finds a cashew. CUT TO BLACK.

114   INT/EXT. FRANK'S SCHOOL - DAY   114

Bernard and Joan stare at MS. LEMON, Frank's principal.

                    BERNARD
          This seems quite impossible.

Joan, stunned, says as if it's happening to someone else:

                    JOAN
          The poor boy.

                    MS. LEMON
          I mean, masturbating is his own issue.
          But Hector witnessed the locker incident
          and then later semen was found in the
          library...

                    BERNARD
          Who's Hector?

Ms. Lemon indicates a CUSTODIAN over to the side, who nods
politely.

                    BERNARD (CONT'D)
          How do you know they were both Frank's.

                                              (CONTINUED)

> MS. LEMON
> Well, I suppose it's possible other kids
> are masturbating and spreading their semen
> around the school as well...possible, yes,
> but also somewhat unlikely.

> BERNARD
> Oh, it happens I'm sure much more than we
> know.

> JOAN
> Bernard, have you ever done something
> like this?

Bernard looks at Ms. Lemon, who nervously looks away, then
back at Joan. He says indignantly:

> BERNARD
> I'm not going to answer that.

> MS. LEMON
> Has anything been going on at home that
> might've provoked this behavior?

> JOAN
> Well, Bernard left him behind for three
> days last week.

> BERNARD
>   (pause)
> And, of course, Frank's mother divorced
> me earlier this year, which might also
> have something to do with it.
>   (suddenly, to Joan)
> Did you tell Frank I'm unattractive?

> JOAN
> No. He just doesn't want your bone
> structure.

They all stare at each other uncomfortably.

115 EXT. FRANK'S SCHOOL - DAY   115

Ms. Lemon holds the front door for Bernard and Joan.

> MS. LEMON
> Ms. Berkman, I read your story in The New
> Yorker. I thought it was quite moving.

STILLS

Family conference

Bernard Berkman (Jeff Daniels)

Joan Berkman (Laura Linney)

Frank Berkman (Owen Kline)

Walt Berkman (Jesse Eisenberg)

Outside Frank's school

At the Bubble

"Walt, did you write that song?"

At Blue Velvet

"Hey You."

Out for Tylenol

Room at Dad's

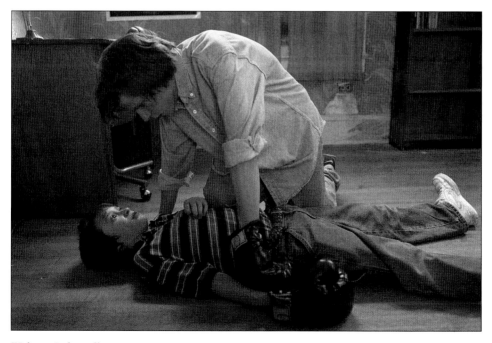

"I hate it here."

Left at home

"What's up, brother?"

Talent show celebration

"I'm your teacher."

Lili's room

"You're cute."

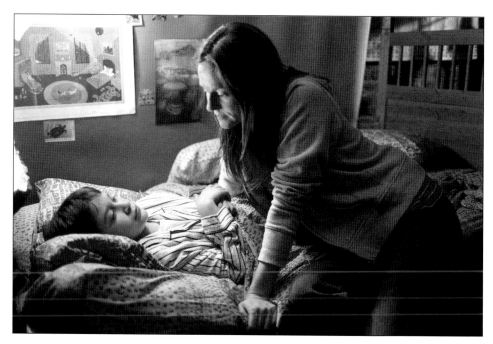

Tucking Frank in

"Good grip, brother."

"He made his own interpretation."

Joan at the window

Double-parked

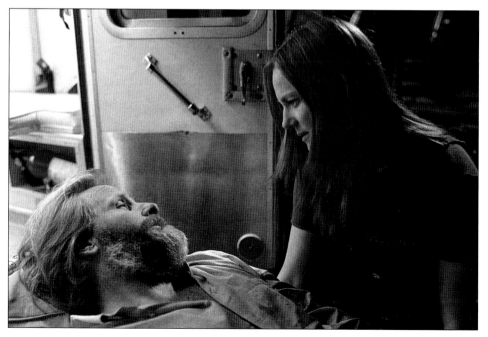

"You're calling me a bitch?"

Frank's room

Noah with Laura

Noah and Wes

Noah with Jeff

Noah and Laura

The American Museum of Natural History

115   CONTINUED:

                        JOAN
             Oh, thanks. Thanks a lot.

Bernard's expression is completely blank. Bernard and Joan
start down the steps to the sidewalk.

                        JOAN (CONT'D)
             You're living with a twenty year old.

                        BERNARD
             It's none of your business, Joan. She's
             older than twenty.

                        JOAN
             It's my business when you have our kids.
             It's confusing for them. Frank says
             Walt's in love with her.

                        BERNARD
                   (hesitates)
             Walt has a girlfriend.
                   (suddenly angry)
             Fuck off, Joan. I don't ask about you
             and Ivan. Stay out of my life. I can't
             believe you'd talk to me like this. You
             left all those fucking ticket stubs and
             letters lying around. You wanted me to
             know. It was fucking torture, Joan.
             Fucking torture.

Pink Floyd's version of "Hey You".

He walks to his car. He gets in, puts the key in the ignition,
but doesn't turn it. He sinks down slightly in his chair.

116   INT. IVAN'S CAR - DAY   116

We FOLLOW Joan as she gets in. Frank sits in the passenger
seat, staring at the floor. She looks at him. Takes a deep
breath. Reaches over and touches his head.

117   INT. HIGHSCHOOL CLASSROOM - DUSK   117

Mr. Simic is now playing the Pink Floyd song for Bernard and
Joan on a tape deck. Bernard reads the liner notes. They sit
at desks across the aisle from each other and listen in
silence. Simic turns it off. Joan absent mindedly peels skin
off her lip.

                                              (CONTINUED)

117   CONTINUED:

> BERNARD
> He made his own interpretation.

> MR. SIMIC
> Well, he's still going to have to give
> the prize money back. But obviously it's
> a bigger problem. He isn't doing any of
> his school work either.

> BERNARD
> His paper on Gatsby was quite brilliant,
> I thought. It's one of his favorite
> books.

> MR. SIMIC
> That may be, but I don't believe he's
> read it.
> (pause)
> You both should talk to him.

Bernard turns to Joan. She's already looking at him. She
flicks some skin off her finger and says sadly:

> JOAN
> I think Bernard has to do it.

118   INT. WALT'S ROOM AT DAD'S - EVENING   118

Bernard stands in the doorway, Walt is on the floor with his
guitar in his lap.

> BERNARD
> He wants you to see a therapist.

> WALT
> I don't need that.

> BERNARD
> That's what I said. Does Simic know both
> your parents have Ph.D.'s in literature?

> WALT
> I've mentioned it.

> BERNARD
> I think he's full of shit. These public
> schools tend to hire well meaning, but
> ultimately unsophisticated bureaucrats.

118   CONTINUED:

                        WALT
          Yeah. I don't like him.

                        BERNARD
          But you might have to do it. Just to
          please the school.

                        WALT
          I don't need it.

                        BERNARD
          I know. And unfortunately probably a guy
          with a BA in psychology. Not a real
          shrink.

119   INT. SCHOOL THERAPIST'S OFFICE - DAY   119

      Walt sits across from the therapist, MR. WADDLES, 30's, who
      is already answering a question of Walt's.

                        MR. WADDLES
          I have an MA in Developmental Psychology
          from the Yale Child Studies Program.

                        WALT
          Did you get a PhD?

                        MR. WADDLES
          No, an MA is a masters.

                        WALT
          Uh huh. Right.

                        MR. WADDLES
          Do you have any thoughts about why you're
          here, Walt?

                        WALT
          Not really.

                        MR. WADDLES
          Nothing?

                        WALT
          No.

      Waddles waits a moment, consults his notes.

119 CONTINUED:

                    MR. WADDLES
          You said you wrote the song you played in
          assembly.

                    WALT
          Uh huh.

                    MR. WADDLES
          Why?

                    WALT
          I don't know.

                    MR. WADDLES
          Did you have a reason?

                    WALT
          I felt I could've written it.

                    MR. WADDLES
          Okay. But you didn't. It was written by
          Roger Waters of Pink Floyd. I think you
          know that.

                    WALT
          Yes, but I felt I could've so the fact
          that it was already written was kind of a
          technicality.

                    MR. WADDLES
          I see.
              (pause)
          I can imagine this is a little
          uncomfortable for you to talk about.

                    WALT
          I guess. It's hard to explain.

Silence.

                    MR. WADDLES
          I wonder how you're feeling right now.

                    WALT
          I don't know.

                    MR. WADDLES
          I'd like to know more about you. Why
          don't you tell me about something less
          uncomfortable. A nice memory maybe.

>   WALT
> Isn't that kind of a stock question for a
> shrink?

>   MR. WADDLES
> Yes, that's more or less how this works.

>   WALT
> I can't think of anything right now.

>   MR. WADDLES
> Just think.

>   WALT
> Come on...

>   MR. WADDLES
> Just something. Meet me half way here.

A silence as Walt thinks.

>   WALT
> Umm...let's see...okay, when I was around
> six, my Mom and I...she and I ducked out
> of Julie Glynn's birthday party to watch
> "Robin Hood" together on our TV.

>   MR. WADDLES
> That sounds like a nice memory.

>   WALT
> I liked Errol Flynn.

>   MR. WADDLES
> Errol Flynn. That's all?

>   WALT
> And I was glad she let me leave the party
> early to watch the movie. She and I
> loved that movie. It's like...we were
> pals then...we'd do things together...
> we'd look at the knight armor at the Met.
> The scary fish at the Natural History
> Museum. I was always afraid of the squid
> and whale fighting. I can only look at
> it with my hands in front of my face.
> When we'd get home, after my bath, she'd
> go through all the different things we
> saw that day in the museum.
>   (MORE)

119   CONTINUED: (3)

                         WALT (CONT'D)
          And then we'd get to the squid and whale
          and she'd describe it for me which was
          still scary, but less scary and it was
          fun. It was fun to hear about it.

                         MR. WADDLES
          Did your Dad live at home back then?

                         WALT
          Yeah, why?

                         MR. WADDLES
          You didn't mention him. Where was he
          during all of this?

                         WALT
          He was...I don't know exactly.
          Downstairs maybe. He didn't ever come to
          the museum...This was...It was before my
          brother was born...before...it was
          earlier...

Walt stops for a moment, choked up. He looks at Waddles with
a surprised expression on his face. Waddles gives him a "Not
bad, eh?" shrug.

120   INT. BERNARD'S HOUSE - DAY   120

Walt opens the front door, drops his bookbag on the floor.

                         WALT
              Hello?

No answer. He goes up stairs. Looks in his Dad's room.
It's empty. Walks over to his room, throws his jacket on the
bed. Goes over to Lili's room. The door's ajar. He hears:

                         LILI'S VOICE
              I'm not...not now, Bernard. I'm not
              feeling like it.

                         BERNARD'S VOICE
              Why not?

                         LILI'S VOICE
              I'm just not, okay?

Walt peers in.

121   INT. LILI'S ROOM - CONTINUOUS   121

Bernard has his hand up Lili's shirt, kneading her breast.

>   BERNARD
>   Put me in your mouth.

Lili's eyes meet Walt's over Bernard's shoulder.

>   LILI
>   Walt...hi.

>   WALT
>   Hi.

Bernard turns around to see his son. Walt just stares.

>   BERNARD
>   Hey, Walt.

>   WALT
>   Hi.

>   BERNARD
>   I'll be right there, we can...hang out.

Walt leaves. Lili takes Bernard's hands off her.

>   LILI
>   I don't want to do this anymore.

Lili walks to the other side of the cramped room. Bernard
says nothing, looking both hurt and angry. He walks past her
and down the stairs.

122   INT. BERNARD'S PEUGEOT - DUSK   122

Bernard pulls up to Joan's house.

123   EXT. JOAN'S HOUSE - MOMENTS LATER   123

Bernard rings the bell. Frank opens the door.

>   BERNARD
>   Hi. Is Walt here?

>   FRANK
>   No.

123   CONTINUED:

                    BERNARD
            Oh. I'd like you to come to my house.

                    FRANK
            Isn't it Mom's night?

                    BERNARD
            Yeah, but I'd like you to come over.

                    FRANK
            Umm, I have to put on my shoes. Come in,
            I guess.

Bernard slowly follows him in.

124   INT. JOAN'S LIVING ROOM - CONTINUOUS   124

Bernard reluctantly enters. Frank sits on the floor and
starts putting on his sneakers.

                    BERNARD
            Place looks different.

                    FRANK
            She got some new furniture in Maine.

                    BERNARD
            That was my TV. I bought that TV.

                    FRANK
            Mmm hmm.

Bernard looks at the bookshelf.

                    BERNARD
            That's my Jude The Obscure.

                    FRANK
            You wanna take it?

                    BERNARD
            Nah.

                    FRANK
            She still has some of the books you wrote.

Bernard turns to the ceiling high shelves full of books. His
eyes scan the titles. He finds the books with his name on the
spines. He can't move. His face grows suddenly emotional.

(CONTINUED)

                    FRANK (CONT'D)
         Dad, why are you taking me to your house
         on Mom's night?

                    BERNARD
         Just a minute.

He stands there, motionless, soaking in the place. For a
brief moment, everything softens. His eyes grow watery. He
takes a deep breath. All the change of the last few months
seems to register. Joan enters from the kitchen.

                    JOAN
         Oh...

                    BERNARD
         Hi. Frank let me in. I didn't realize
         you were here.

                    JOAN
         I'm here. It's Monday.

                    BERNARD
         I'd like to take him for just tonight.
         I'll give you two Thursdays in a row or
         something.

                    FRANK
         Mom...

                    JOAN
         It's my night. He wants to stay.

Bernard picks up a little toy soldier off an end table.
Inspects it.

                    JOAN (CONT'D)
         Be careful, that's an antique.

                    BERNARD
         Where's Walt?

                    JOAN
         I don't know where Walt is.

Bernard suddenly starts up the stairs. Joan tenses.

                    JOAN (CONT'D)
         He's not up there, Bernard. He doesn't
         come here.

(CONTINUED)

He stops, remains there for a moment.

>   JOAN (CONT'D)
>   You should go. You'll see them tomorrow.

>   BERNARD
>   (to Frank)
>   Tell Walt to call me.

He comes down the stairs and goes to the door.

125   EXT. HUNAN PALACE - DUSK   125

Walt looks in the window. His gaze goes from family to
family, sharing plates, kids trying to eat with chopsticks.
He finds Sophie and her parents at a table in the back. He
watches for a beat. She suddenly looks up and spots him. He
awkwardly ducks behind a menu that's pasted to the glass. He
waits a moment and peers back out. She's still staring. He
stares back too. Her parents turn and look at him. A
moment. Walt ducks back. He waits. He peeks back out, but
they're not paying attention. He walks away.

126   EXT. PROSPECT PARK - DUSK   126

It's getting darker. Walt runs along the path. He suddenly
darts into the brush, pushing his way through the trees.

He emerges to a pond. No one is around. He walks toward it
and stops. He stares out over the water.

127   INT. BERNARD'S PEUGEOT/EXT. JOAN'S HOUSE - DUSK   127

Bernard sits in his car which is double parked. Starts it
up, changes his mind, and puts it in park. He sees Walt
running up the block. Walt, whose head is soaking wet,
doesn't see Bernard watching.

Bernard waits for Walt to go inside Joan's, gets out of the
car and approaches the house. He wades through the front
garden and crouches down to the basement window. Inside,
Frank, shirtless, sits on his bed with a beer. Bernard taps
on the window. Frank looks up, startled.

128   INT. JOAN'S LIVING ROOM - DUSK   128

Walt walks in, his hair and face wet. Joan enters from the
kitchen. Her face lights up and she goes to hug him, but
backs off just before reaching him, afraid of scaring him off.

                       JOAN
Chicken, what happened?

                       WALT
I dunked my head in that pond in the park.

                       JOAN
The one near the zoo?
    (he nods)
Sweety, that's filthy. I hope you didn't
drink any of it.

Joan retrieves a towel from the bathroom and hands it to Walt.

                       WALT
Some may have got in my mouth. I tried
not to swallow.
    (pause)
I shouldn't've broken up with Sophie.

                       JOAN
Why did you?

                       WALT
I thought I could do better.

                       JOAN
Better how?

Walt gives this some thought. His answer comes as a surprise
to him.

                       WALT
I don't know.

                       JOAN
That's good you miss her.

                       WALT
Yeah, but I don't see myself as a person
who is in this situation. I just don't.
You know, I thought this could've been a
real thing. A real love affair. I don't
see myself this way.

                       JOAN
Well, this is how it is.

(CONTINUED)

>   WALT
>   Did you ever love Dad? Cause if you
>   didn't, why did you ever marry him? If
>   you were going to leave him, why did you
>   put us all through this.
>
>   JOAN
>   It wasn't planned. When we first met, he
>   was unlike anyone. In Columbus there was
>   no one like your Dad. We were on the
>   Ohio State campus and we'd take our
>   sandwiches out to the green and picnic
>   together. He asked me who I preferred:
>   Antonioni or Fellini. I said Antonioni
>   which was the right answer, I guess, at
>   the time.
>
>   WALT
>   Is it Fellini now?
>
>   JOAN
>   I don't know. I think it's whoever you
>   like better.

They make eye contact for a second.

>   JOAN (CONT'D)
>   I had had an affair with a man before
>   your father. He worked in the college
>   bookstore. We used to make love in the
>   stock room. It got so that the smell of
>   text books made me think of him.
>
>   WALT
>   Mom, I don't want to hear about your
>   affairs, please.
>
>   JOAN
>   I'm sorry. I think I don't know what I
>   can say to you.
>
>   WALT
>   You have a way of saying things sometimes
>   that are a way I don't want to hear them.
>   Children shouldn't hear these things from
>   their Moms. You should particularly
>   watch it around Frank.

(CONTINUED)

                    JOAN
        I know, chicken, it's something I do.
        It's a bad habit.

                    WALT
        Do you...do you remember when we watched
        "Robin Hood"?

        A moment, Joan jumps. Walt, startled, turns. Frank and
        Bernard stand in the doorway.

                    FRANK
        He knocked on my window.

                    JOAN
        Bernard, what are you doing?

                    BERNARD
        Joan, let me ask you something. All that
        work I did at the end of our marriage,
        making dinners, cleaning up, being more
        attentive. It never was going to make a
        difference, was it? You were leaving no
        matter what...

                    JOAN
        You never made a dinner.

                    BERNARD
        I made burgers the time you had
        pneumonia.

                    JOAN
        Only after I insisted!

                    BERNARD
        Well, if I had made more dinners would
        that've made a difference?

                    JOAN
        I was ready to leave a long time ago. I
        just didn't know it then.

                    BERNARD
                (hesitates)
        I've been giving it some thought. I
        mean, you called my father at the last
        minute. You said something. Whatever
        you said, he thought I could save the
        marriage.

                                              (CONTINUED)

128   CONTINUED: (4)

Bernard and Walt quickly meet eyes.

                    BERNARD (CONT'D)
          You felt I wasn't aggressive enough. I'll
          make more of an effort to do stuff. I've
          been cooking and doing chores at my house.
          I make veal cutlets which the boys love.

Frank looks at his father as if to say, "What are you talking
about?"

                    BERNARD (CONT'D)
          Why don't we all have dinner and talk
          more about this.

Joan starts to laugh. It catches her off guard. It's
clearly out of her control. She tries to stop, she sucks it
in, but it erupts to a hysterical level. The two boys and
Bernard watch her as she continues to shake and laugh.
Nobody says anything. Finally it dies down. She wipes the
tears from her eyes. Coughs. She's exhausted.

                    JOAN
          I'm sorry... It's just...burgers...once.

Joan loses it again, laughing, but struggles to control
herself. Bernard sighs, saddened by this. But as it sinks
in, he just grows angry.

                    BERNARD
          I'll sue you, Joan. You know I will.
          You had an affair for four years with
          that fucking shrink that ruined our
          marriage and I can get the kids. I
          talked to Eddie Goodman, who works on
          these cases all the time and I have an
          open and shut case.
               (pause)
          Frank, Walt, get in the car.

A pause.

                    JOAN
          Sue me? That's so...I can't... You only
          wanted joint custody cause you pay less
          child support that way. Because it was
          cheaper for you.

Joan stops herself. She pounds the top of the TV with her
fist, upset she said what she did.

                                        (CONTINUED)

Walt looks at his Dad, "Is this true?". Bernard goes to the
front door and opens it. Street noise enters the house.

                    BERNARD
          Walt, Frank!

                    FRANK
          I don't want to go.

                    BERNARD
          I don't give a shit. Frank, get in the
          car.

Frank doesn't move.

                    BERNARD (CONT'D)
          Frank!

Bernard grabs Frank's arm. Frank bursts into tears. Walt
steps between them.

                    WALT
          Let him stay.

                    BERNARD
          I'm just asking this one thing.

                    WALT
          He wants to stay. Let him. I'll go.

Frank and Walt meet eyes. Frank's nose is running, tears
streaming down his face. Bernard turns to Walt.

                    BERNARD
          Fine.

Frank and Walt stare at one another for an extended moment.

                    FRANK
          Hold on...

Frank kneels down, picks up the CAT and hands him to Walt.

                    FRANK (CONT'D)
          You want him tonight?

                    WALT
          Okay. Thanks.

                    FRANK
          That's alright, my brother.

Bernard and Walt walk out the front door.

129 EXT. JOAN'S HOUSE - DUSK   129

Just as they step outside, the cat leaps out of Walt's arms
and into the street. Joan screams.

> JOAN
> The cat!

It runs under a parked car. Bernard and Walt go after it,
surrounding the car, Bernard taking the street side and Walt
the curb. They both kneel down and look under the vehicle.
The cat mews from beneath it. Bernard reaches under and
grabs its tail. He and Walt meet eyes underneath the car.

> BERNARD
> I got him. Joan, I got him! I got him!

He turns to Joan and Frank who watch from the stoop. His
attention goes to a COP next to his double parked car,
writing a ticket.

> BERNARD (CONT'D)
> Goddammit!

Bernard releases the cat who darts down the block and out of
sight.

> WALT
> Dad!

Bernard rises and starts toward the Cop.

> BERNARD
> I'm moving it!

A car SCREECHES on the breaks and swerves just avoiding
Bernard. The Cop looks up. The DRIVER yells, furious.

> DRIVER
> What's your problem?

> BERNARD
> (under his breath)
> Fuck off.

Ivan walks down the block toward them. He starts to pick up
the pace. Walt turns to Frank who has wandered closer.

129   CONTINUED:

                           WALT
                 Did you see him go?

Frank shakes his head, No and bursts into more tears.

                           JOAN
                 Frank, go inside. Where is he?

                           WALT
                 I don't know where he went.

Bernard reaches the Cop. His face red, he's panting. The
Driver continues to shout at him. Ivan jogs over to the
scene.

                           IVAN
                 What's going on?

                           BERNARD
                 I had him.

Bernard's breaths are audible, deep. He looks at the Cop. The
Driver curses. Ivan next to him. Joan and his kids. He
suddenly clutches his arm. And falls. Ivan drops to his side.

                           IVAN
                 Bernard? Are you okay, man?
                      (pause)
                 Joan, call an ambulance!

Joan runs inside. Frank stares at Bernard. Walt races over
and kneels down to his father. Bernard squints at Walt.

                           BERNARD
                 Walt, get in the car.

130   EXT. BROOKLYN STREET - NIGHT   130

Bernard, awake, on a stretcher, is about to be loaded onto the
back of an ambulance. Joan and Frank wait on the corner.
Bernard says something to the PARAMEDICS and they stop for a
moment as Bernard waves for Joan to come over. She approaches
and leans down to him. He runs his thumb over his lips and
looks at her.

                           BERNARD
                 "Degeulasse".

                           JOAN
                 What?

                                                    (CONTINUED)

He starts to repeat the gesture, but stops self-consciously.

                        BERNARD
It means, "Bitch". Don't you remember?

                        JOAN
You're calling me a bitch?

                        BERNARD
No, don't you remember the last line in
Godard's "A Bout de Soufle". Belmondo
calls Seberg a bitch. "Degeulasse". We
saw it at the Thalia with the Dicksteins.
I got you in for a children's price. You
were pregnant with Walt.

                        JOAN
             (long pause)
Like six weeks.

                        BERNARD
I still got you in for a children's
ticket. You told me you didn't like
Godard. You thought the jump cuts--

Bernard is suddenly thrust up in the air on the gurney and
rolled inside.

                    BERNARD (CONT'D)
I'd check for the cat behind the ashcans
under the Golodner's stoop!

                        JOAN
Okay.

They meet eyes briefly. He gives a "Who would've thought"
kind of shrug. She nods. Ivan and Walt climb into the back
with Bernard and the door is shut.

The ambulance pulls away. Silence. Joan and Frank start
walking, surveying the block for the missing cat. Frank is a
bit stunned, his face smeared from crying.

                        FRANK
Do you think we'll find him?

                        JOAN
I hope so.

(CONTINUED)

                    FRANK
        Do you think one day we could go to the
        Galapagos?

                    JOAN
        I don't know, Pickle.
            (pause)
        Ivan and I could take you to the country
        on Saturday to see some real turtles.

                    FRANK
        Saturday's Dad's day.

We see them from a distance, alone on an empty street.

131 INT. AMBULANCE - NIGHT   131

The siren wails. Walt and Ivan sit in silence. Bernard is
sedated in the back, a paramedic at his side.

                    WALT
        I didn't write it.

                    IVAN
        I know.

                    WALT
        Pink Floyd did.

                    IVAN
        It's okay, brother.

132 INT. HOSPITAL ROOM - MORNING   132

Walt peers in. His Dad lies on a bed, looking pale and thin,
reading a detective novel. Bernard looks up, sees Walt and
smiles sheepishly.

                    BERNARD
        There's my son.

                    WALT
        Hey. Are you okay?

                    BERNARD
        I'm fine. Thought it was a heartattack,
        but I think I'm just exhausted. Doctor
        said I'm exhausted.

                        WALT
          Too many veal cutlets?

                        BERNARD
               (smiles)
          Maybe.

                        WALT
          Is that a good book?

                        BERNARD
          Oh...this is pulp...it's not serious...
          it's...you know it's hard to read a good
          book in the hospital. But this isn't bad
          of its kind. Leonard is the filet of the
          crime genre.

Walt is silent.

                        BERNARD (CONT'D)
          I'd like you to stay here for the day. I
          need the company.

                        WALT
               (pause)
          Okay.

                        BERNARD
          Lili moved out.

Bernard gives a "What can you do?" raise of his eyebrows.
Walt nods.

                        BERNARD (CONT'D)
          Do me a favor, go out in the hall and get
          me another pillow, my neck is hurting.

Walt doesn't move. Silence.

                        WALT
          Dad, you know how for my birthday you
          gave me Nikes.

                        BERNARD
          What?

                        WALT
          How you gave me my Nikes as a birthday
          gift?

                    BERNARD
I wanted to get you something you could
use.

                    WALT
I know, but you know, since Mom gets me
winter coats and you get me sneakers as
part of your divorce...anyway...

                    BERNARD
In our separation agreement, it says I'm
responsible for sneakers up to fifty
dollars, those Nikes were over eighty.

                    WALT
Uh huh.

                    BERNARD
And I don't think you told me anything
else specific that you wanted.

                    WALT
I know, I should've thought of some things.

                    BERNARD
You actually get more presents now since
you get them from both your mother and me.
When we were together we gave them jointly.

                    WALT
I know.
            (flustered)
And I like the sneakers so it doesn't
really matter. I'm not really angry
anymore. It's just...what bothers me is
you didn't...You didn't try to...

He trails off. A moment as Bernard takes this in.

                    BERNARD
I got you the sneakers.

                    WALT
            (takes a deep breath)
Maybe we could even things out a bit and
I could stay at Mom's a few extra days
since I've been staying more at yours...

                       BERNARD
It's not a good time right now, I'm not
going to be a hundred percent for a
while. I'd like you around.

                       WALT
I don't think I want to come for a while.

                       BERNARD
It's not up to you, Walt. You're a
minor. You're in my custody. My home is
your home too.

                       WALT
I'm not coming.

                       BERNARD
Why?

Walt is about to say something. He doesn't.

                     BERNARD (CONT'D)
That hurts my feelings.

Walt looks surprised.

                     BERNARD (CONT'D)
Don't be difficult. If you like, we can
get you some more posters or make your
room better, paint it a different color.
I got Frank a turtle.
          (indicating his blazer on the
          back of the chair)
Look in the pocket of my jacket.

Walt walks over to the coat, he feels in the pockets. He
removes a few little pieces of broken green clay.

                     BERNARD (CONT'D)
The guy said that was the best one. It's
got a blue dot on it or something that
makes it worth more.

Walt holds it out to Bernard.

                     BERNARD (CONT'D)
Mmm. I guess it didn't survive the fall.

Walt looks at the shards and dust in his hand.

                                                BERNARD (CONT'D)
                    We won't tell Frank.

                                                WALT
                    No.

Tears suddenly stream down Walt's face.

                                      WALT (CONT'D)
                    He would've liked it.

                                          BERNARD
                    I could lend you my first edition of The
                    Naked and The Dead.
                        (pause)
                    As a present.

                                                WALT
                    Let me get you a pillow.

Walt goes out the door in the hallway. He pauses for a
moment, removes a pillow off a gurney and brings it back into
the room. Bernard awkwardly lifts his head and Walt jams the
pillow under his Dad's neck. Bernard tries not to look at his
son's crying, he presses the nurse button a few times, but
doesn't seem convinced it's working. He finally looks at
Walt, moved himself. Bernard's voice cracks as he says:

                                            BERNARD
                    You used to be very emotional when you
                    were younger.

Walt nods.

                                      BERNARD (CONT'D)
                    Did I look pretty silly out there,
                    falling on the concrete?

                                              WALT
                      (pause)
                    Yeah.

Bernard bursts into laughter. Walt watches him curiously.

                                        WALT (CONT'D)
                    What are you laughing at?

                                              BERNARD
                    That was funny how you said, "Yeah".
                    Good comic timing.

                                                     (CONTINUED)

132   CONTINUED: (5)

                         WALT
               Thanks.

Bernard smiles at him warmly. He reaches out his hand. Walt
takes it. Bernard squeezes it.

                         BERNARD
               Why don't we get some breakfast. See if
               you can find the nurse out there.

Walt starts for the door.

                         BERNARD (CONT'D)
               Try to get the blonde, she looks like a
               young Monica Vitti.

Walt nods, turns and goes out the door.

133   INT. HOSPITAL HALLWAY - CONTINUOUS   133

Walt walks down the hall a bit. A Chinese NURSE approaches.
He stops in front of her. She looks at him. Silence. She
waits for him to say something.

                         WALT
               Excuse me. The man in that room wants to
               order some breakfast.

                         NURSE
               Okay.

Walt watches her disappear into Bernard's room. Pause. He
walks in the other direction. We FOLLOW him as he passes a
blonde Italian-looking nurse, goes by Ivan in the waiting
room, reaches the elevators, presses the button. He goes for
the stairs.

134   INT. HOSPITAL STAIRWELL - CONTINUOUS   134

He jogs down the stairs, clutching the rail.

135   EXT. HOSPITAL - MORNING   135

And now he's outside. Morning rush. A crowded sidewalk. He
walks briskly for a bit. Turns a corner, keeps going.

136   EXT. CENTRAL PARK WEST - MORNING   136

He walks, head down. He looks up. The Museum of Natural
History. It's just opening for the day.

137   INT. MUSEUM OF NATURAL HISTORY - MOMENTS LATER   137

Walt enters the room with the big whale hanging from the
ceiling. He looks at the dioramas. Finding the one with the
squid and the whale he mentioned to the shrink earlier. He
approaches it a bit warily. It's dark and scary. He gazes
into the black, finding the squid and then the whale. We
STAY on his face as he takes this in. Very slowly, he leans
his head against the glass. And rests.

CUT TO BLACK

SCENE NOTES

BY NOAH BAUMBACH

In the finished film there are several line edits within scenes that I haven't noted here. I've focused instead on changes or thoughts that tie into the bigger picture.

Additionally, the major cuts and reshuffling of scenes occur in the beginning of the film.

Scene 2: I imagined a lot of this film at dusk. The idea was that it took place during that time after school, but before dinner. A time when, as a kid, I put off doing my homework and watched *Three's Company* reruns and *Live at Five*.

Scene 3: In the script, this scene was important because it showed us how Frank was picking up clues—he recognizes on some level that things are not as they seem. And Joan isn't prepared to discuss anything specific with him. It also raised the word "divorce." When people read the script, it framed things for them; it announced the issues we were going to face for the next hundred or so pages. We shot this scene and it played great.

But, once I assembled the tennis game (Scene 1), I realized pretty quickly that I didn't need this bedroom exchange. The tennis played so effectively and demonstrated so much of what was going on with the Berkmans that it allowed me to remove the Joan/Frank scene and the following Walt/Sophie party. It enabled me to speed up and, subsequently, discover the pace of the entire movie.

In a sense, the script revealed things more gently while the finished movie throws you right into the fray.

I moved Scene 15 here to replace the missing 4 and 5.

Scene 4: We shot this scene, but I cut it out almost immediately. In the script, the Orson Welles discussion set up Walt nicely: his way of taking his father's opinions and passing them off as his own. The party also introduced Sophie. In the cut, it felt a little off-topic. The family was the focus. And we could just as easily bring Sophie in later. I missed the Welles dialogue, but I got over that.

Scene 5: Originally the party took place indoors and then spilled out into the street. I collapsed the two scenes to one in the living room to make it more economical to shoot. This scene was not fun to do. It was the half-way point of a very short shooting schedule—23 days—it was pouring rain and the line producer was making me anxious about overtime. It didn't turn out as well as I had hoped.

Scene 8: We initially planned to shoot this, but didn't. Our schedule was so tight and had no margin for error, so I had to make some difficult decisions on the go. Cutting this was a relatively easy one. Initially I thought it might be good to set up the spectre of the talent show early on, but Walt mentions it again in Scene 12 to his mother and father. Tony talks about his puppets here, and in the movie, we do get to see the end of his act at the talent show. The prop master, Jeff Butcher, did such a good job with the papier-mâché, I didn't want the puppets to go to waste.

Scene 13: I had to extend Lili's story to accommodate the camera pan we designed for the shot.

Scene 15: My girlfriend, Jennifer, suggested I move this family dinner earlier to immediately follow the tennis game. Once we did this it helped the beginning of the movie enormously. It's an effectively quiet companion scene to the louder, frenetic tennis match. In the script, it was a tense dinner coming after Walt and Bernard had just seen Joan on the street with another man. Here it's a tense dinner following a tense tennis game. Again, the script had a slower burn so that this scene felt appropriate coming on page 15. In the movie, things were happening faster.

Scene 30: We shot the dialogue at the top of the scene with the kids and it was funny, but there was too much preamble. In the movie we come in on "Joint custody blows." I wanted to stay in the throes of the Berkman separation. Also we didn't have permits to shoot on the subway, so much of this was shot in—I guess you'd call it—a guerilla style. We couldn't control when trains rumbled in. Sound was tricky.

Scene 31: This scene kept getting pushed to later and later on the schedule. So much so I realized we didn't need it.

Scene 32: In the edit, I moved this scene ahead to Scene 41. Again, the divorce was the story, and I felt this took us away from where we needed to be. This allowed us to get to Bernard's new house sooner.

I originally put Walt and Sophie's exchange in the midst of a dance class because I had been roped into a dance class as a kid and I liked the setting. This scene was to be shot the same day as the earlier party, but we never got to it. (See notes on Scenes 4-5). The scene was necessary, so I moved the location to a chemistry classroom because we were going to be shooting at the high school the following week. At the time I was very unhappy about this because I had a lot of ideas for the dance visuals. But since I ended up cutting the earlier Sophie scene at the party and moving this one to a later point, the classroom turned out to be a more appropriate location. It's now our introduction to Sophie, and it grounds their meeting in the everyday.

Scene 37: We shot the cat pissing. Actually, a simulation of the cat pissing because you can't get a cat to piss on command. Maybe you can with a studio budget, but on an indie, it has to be faked. Anyway, I cut it—it didn't look great.

Scene 39: Warner Bros. wanted six grand for the use of the *Blow Up* image. New Yorker Films gave us *The Mother and the Whore* for free.

Scene 41: I originally had a quick shot of Bernard looking up the stairs to see what was going on. In the movie, we go directly to Walt and Sophie in the classroom.

Scene 48: The last third of this scene was cut for pace reasons.

Scene 60–62: This was cut before it was shot. It's cute, but I had a lot to cover at the high school and not a lot of time.

Scene 63: The extras casting director sent us an eight-year-old girl to play Wendy Chen. We found someone taking a summer school class at the high school and cast her instead.

Scene 66: The kids are what brought me into the story, but in later drafts of the script I attacked things from the parents' perspective. I had originally envisioned scenes that only Frank and Walt could have witnessed, but the more I lived with the script, the more I found this limiting. I initially wrote this scene between Joan and Bernard as an exercise; it was a way to break the constraints I had put on myself. Now, I can't imagine the movie without it. I mention this also because I love how Jeff and Laura played it.

Scene 68: Again, six grand to use a poster! *The Mother and the Whore* was free.

Scene 73: I'm not sure what this "Omitted" refers to. We always cut right to the movie screen.

Scene 81: More patter with the kids that I cut down.

Scene 87: I cut Otto's last line because it referred to a previous discussion that was no longer in the movie.

Scene 90: Initially Walt and Sophie celebrated a one-month anniversary in her parents' dining room and gave each other gifts. Sophie gave Walt *This Side of Paradise* and Walt gave her his dad's novel *Under Water*. Walt then bullied Sophie about making out with another classmate. I decided to collapse these two locations into one scene and one room. I moved the dialogue about Nelson Barton to the end of Scene 91 and cut the exchange of presents.

Scene 96: I thought it would be stronger to go right to Frank in the hallway. We've already seen him in the library; we know what's going on.

Scene 97: For some reason I imagined a Dissolve here. I didn't end up using any Dissolves. I was never even tempted.

Scene 98: Once you only have a million and a half to make the movie and twenty-three days to shoot it, you regret describing any scene as "packed with students." We did our best to make the auditorium look full.

Scene 100: I was told it would be too expensive to light the whole outside of the high school, so we compromised and shot in the stairwell, but with the night exterior visible outside the open door.

Scene 102: I cut the last few exchanges here. It was stronger to go from "things might change for you" to Walt and Sophie in the following scene.

Scene 108: We didn't shoot this. I made a decision not to use any transition shots.

Scene 119: Initially there was reference in the dialogue to a Mr. Waddles, but I took that out, so he's credited as "School Therapist" in the movie. I worked on this scene right up until we started filming. The therapist's question: "Did your dad live at home back then?" came late in the game.

Scene 129: The cat would not run down the stairs. This was the only time during the shoot where I felt real panic. I didn't know what to do. If that cat didn't run, we would have no way to get to the next scene. It was after something like take eleven when the cat wrangler told me she had a "running cat" that looked identical. Needless to say, the running cat is called that for a reason.

Scene 131: I took out Ivan's last line because I didn't want reassurance; I wanted to keep things suspended.

Scene 132: A note I kept hearing from financiers and actors while we tried to get the movie financed was, "Where is Bernard's redemption?" The answer was, "Not in this movie." That said, I added the exchange with Walt about the broken turtle as an attempt to soften Bernard slightly. I'm not sure if it made a difference in the script or not, but once I cut the film, I lifted it immediately. My first instinct was correct. Jeff never gave a shit about redemption either, and I love him for that.

I also took out the bit about the Nikes. I like this dialogue, but in the context of the film it felt petty.

Scene 137: When they renovated this room at the American Museum of Natural History they removed the glass from this diorama. We could've tried to reinsert glass, but we didn't have a lot of time to shoot and there was a plaque that would've made it awkward for Jesse to lean forward. I feel indebted to the museum for letting us film there.

Q & A

WITH NOAH BAUMBACH
BY ROB FELD

*O*n August 5, 2005, Rob Feld met Noah Baumbach for lunch at Bar Pitti in New York's Greenwich Village.

So, first, tell me why we're here at this restaurant.

Noah Baumbach: This is a restaurant that I love. And Wes and I wrote *The Life Aquatic* here. He and I never discussed it, but in retrospect I think we wanted to create the same atmosphere of our friendship in a work environment. So we would come here for lunch every day, basically have the "friend lunch" and then segue into the work afternoon. We would pretty much spend the whole day here, sometimes through dinner. We'd find ourselves ordering again, and then the coffees and wine would come out....

So that's where some of those scenes came from.

NB: Yeah, exactly. We used to joke that, as in *The Usual Suspects*, you could probably find evidence of the entire movie on wine bottles, the menu, and the waiters' names.

Your films are very location-specific. Whether it's Brooklyn or even the dreamland of **Life Aquatic,** *your locations can become characters in and of themselves. How do you think about the environments your characters inhabit?*

NB: I guess I do like to put myself in a familiar area and to invent out of that. Subsequently, the location becomes a character, I guess, but I don't think of it consciously. When we first showed *The Squid and the Whale* at Sundance, people said, "Oh, what a love letter to Brooklyn." I was very glad people felt that, but I never would have thought, "This is my love letter to Brooklyn."

It's interesting because I wrote *Kicking and Screaming* specifically with an East Coast, liberal arts college in mind—I'd gone to Vassar and come up with the story with a friend of mine, Bo Berkman, who went to the Rhode Island School of Design. So there was a sense of not Ivy League, but a good northeastern, liberal arts school. But, for financial and other particulars, we ended up shooting in L.A. It did put a lot of restrictions on the camera—you couldn't dolly too far or you'd get a palm tree. Most people I talk to don't notice, but I can tell because of the light. If you spend enough time in L.A. you can recognize it. Shooting *Kicking and Screaming* became about making it in some nondescript place, which, in a way, is what writing with Wes is like, too. The action in *Life Aquatic* occurs in a place *like* a place, but not in a *specific* real-world place.

With *The Squid and the Whale* it was very different because it couldn't have been shot anywhere except Brooklyn. It was very much about the specificity of an actual place and time. We had a very low budget so there were different constraints. We had to worry about period detail.

Then does creating the physicality of it come more during the directing stage than the writing? Is that when you start working out those details?

NB: It's always in your head, developing, even if you don't write every detail into the script. There are things I let slide on my first two movies that I didn't on this one. All that stuff resonates, whether it's as literal as somebody saying, "I know that block," or "I had that exact picture in my home," or if it's a more abstract feeling—like an emotional connection to a color. And if no one else notices it, I will.

Tell me where **Kicking and Screaming** *came from. What did you study at Vassar?*

NB: I was an English major, but I had already wanted to make movies. I grew up seeing a lot of movies, and movies were talked about a good deal in my family. When I made *Kicking and Screaming*, it, on one hand, seemed like a perfectly natural experience: *Now I'm doing what I wanted to do.* For that very reason, though, it also seemed completely alien. Now I'm actually *making* the movie and it's not exactly what I pictured. I think it was a headier experience than I let on to myself at the time, to have something like that happen so quickly.

Many of the characters in your films, and even the "Shouts & Murmurs" pieces you've done for **The New Yorker,** *share this sense of lost or wasted potential, as though they are constantly thrown by the way reality thwarts their views of who and what they thought they were supposed to be. They're mostly of a certain intelligence, background, and education, and feel a pressure to be something, whatever that may be, and seem shocked when reality doesn't just proffer up that birthright automatically.*

NB: I actually became very interested in Eric Rohmer's movies a few years ago for that very reason—I feel like he's made a version of the same movie over and over again, but I find each one riveting. I didn't initially. I found them difficult at first, but then I saw a whole bunch at once, and really got into the rhythm. They're so much about people's ideas of themselves versus who they really are or what they could be. I'm fascinated by that in my own work, too: people's expectations of themselves and others and their subsequent feelings of disappointment and failure. What drives them or what prevents them from taking risks.

The result is frequently paralyzed people, certainly in **Kicking and Screaming.** *I'm interested in how you construct a compelling story and maintain tension with such characters, who don't necessarily do very much, and where the conflict is mostly internal.*

NB: I taught a screenwriting class at Vassar a few years ago. The first script everyone tends to write is one act stretched out for an entire movie. There's a feeling when you're starting out that movies have a lot less story in them than they actually do, so you write that first screenplay and figure the last 50 pages will kind of take care of themselves. *Kicking and Screaming* is, in a way, that movie. But there is a built-in tension: These people have graduated college, but they haven't left. So every banal conversation is underscored with a sadness and an absurdity to some degree.

Certainly not everything I write is as much about hanging out as that movie was, but it was also what my life was at that time. I was very familiar with it. That said, I do think I am interested in fractured emotional states creating narrative, or at least having an effect on it.

I always resist movies with a pitch line like, "Because of *the bet*, he's got to win the woman by Saturday..." or, "If he can get to this point in time, he'll inherit...*whatever*," which I guess is an excuse to make the middle part of the movie—the human interaction—interesting to people. I'm more interested in the middle part without that contrivance thrown on top of it. I'd like to make that messier stuff compelling. I would hope, if it's done well, the result is even more identifiable because the audience doesn't have to bite off on some ridiculous premise. I don't know anybody in the real world who makes elaborate bets that change their lives, you know? If those people exist, I don't want to know them.

What is the challenge of the middle of the film and how do you overcome it?

NB: I try not to think of the movie conceptually. I start with characters and conversations I find interesting. The story generally comes later. This can be kind of frustrating. I'm sometimes impatient when I'm writing and wish the story would reveal itself more quickly, but the more I know myself and my way of working, I just have to force myself to write through it. I don't want to make the process sound too mysterious. I mean, I have ideas for where a story is going, but I try to let the story and characters evolve and allow for things to turn out differently than I expected.

I've tried the other way. I've tried to come up with some funny premise and then write characters to fit it, and it never works for me.

Was that what **Mr. Jealousy** *was?*

NB: On one hand that movie was an advance for me because I felt more in charge of the visual. I think I've always been pretty good with actors, but I felt like I could communicate things more fluidly and, in a lot of ways, felt like I had taken what I'd learned from *Kicking and Screaming* and improved upon it. That said, I think I made a less good movie, partly because I do think I got a little too caught up in the premise of it, which I thought was clever at the time. All I can really say is, I wouldn't do it the same way now.

So no outline chiseled in stone?

NB: I don't outline. And when I've done jobs either in television or for a studio, and outlines have been part of the deal, it seems completely artificial to me and, I think, made it harder for me to write the script afterward.

I hate that phrase, **it's a very personal story**—*I guess everything is— but* **Kicking and Screaming, Mr. Jealousy,** *and* **The Squid and the Whale** *all seem to chart where you were in your life at a certain point, or I imagine you might be reflecting upon at a certain age.* **Kicking and Screaming** *was absolutely of that moment. Was* **The Life Aquatic** *something of a relief, or nice change of pace, to be pulled out of a place where you have to mine everything yourself?*

NB: Yes. There was never any question it was a movie for Wes to make, and my job was to integrate with that world, to bolster and contribute to it. That said, I fought for the things that I believed in and I thought could work in that environment. I had written *Squid* at this point and was waiting to get the financing for it, so in a lot of ways, it was a relief and a real pleasure to play over at someone else's house. On the flip side, I think Wes had a similar experience producing *Squid*.

So what was your process of writing together, as you sat here at the restaurant?

NB: Wes likes to write everything down by hand, which I think influences the pace and the feel of the movie in an interesting way. We would discuss it and Wes would then, if something seemed right to him, write it down. He'd type up what he wrote and bring in the pages. We'd both take them home, think, and come back in.

How do you usually think about and approach dialogue?

NB: I have conversations with myself. Both in my head and out loud and I write it as I think it. I'm very taken with patterns of talking. Things get shaped and moved around later, but I try to assimilate the sloppiness of how people speak. Or at least how they talk in my head.

Am I wrong to identify a certain sense of tragedy or impending doom in so much of your work, even though you basically work in comedy? Depressed people facing failure, certainly in Kicking and Screaming? Zissou coming to terms with his own mortality? Bernard, in Squid and the Whale, passing on his "standards" and ideas of success, and perhaps inevitable frustration, to his eldest son?

NB: I do feel like everything I write and subsequently make is, in some ways, sadder than I ever intended. Not that I think I'm making broad comedies or anything, but my initial experience of the characters is often one that makes me laugh. I think the interactions in *Squid and the Whale* or in *Kicking and Screaming* are amusing, but at the same time, because they're treated realistically, maybe they can't help but feel sad.

But returning to this idea of expectations, I do think I am very interested in people who have ideas about their lives—who they are and where they're going—and no matter what happens to them, no matter how bad or great things turn out, anything that falls short of their fantasy is going to be a disappointment. Maybe that's what you're picking up on.

Zissou's had a pretty good run, yet he feels like a complete failure. And I've read descriptions of Bernard where it's, "A once great novelist, his best books now behind him..." and my feeling is, we don't know if that's true. It's his idea of success that's much more crippling than any real things that are happening to him. I mean, he's doing okay. He lives in a house, he's got a teaching job. Certainly he's going through a hard time both personally and professionally, but I'm not sure Bernard would be satisfied under rosier conditions. Now that I'm saying it, it all sounds very sad....

Isn't that a compelling, classic idea in both drama and comedy, the way in which we undo ourselves? Your characters seem to have everything going for them but for some reason can't be satisfied or happy. In **Squid and the Whale,** *Walt's smart and can play guitar. He didn't have to claim to have written "Hey You." And holding Sophie up to some bizarre, undefined standard?*

NB: Walt's going out with somebody who he clearly cares about, who cares about him, but she's not his fantasy. Which, of course, nobody is. Bernard tells him, she's good for *now*. You know? As opposed to when? What's later?

Squid and the Whale *is a departure for you in terms of tone. Can you tell me where it came from and what your process was developing it?*

NB: Like I was saying earlier, I left college with this idea that I wanted to make films. Then, suddenly, I was making films, but then had to acknowledge that I wasn't exactly sure what kind of films I wanted to make—which was a strange position to be in. My feeling about *Squid and Whale* is that it's the movie I always wanted to make that I didn't know I was going to make.

It was probably around 2000, I was trying to work on a script that I had initially sold as a pitch, and I was having a hell of a time. Going back to our outlining discussion, I couldn't write what I'd pitched. It seemed forced and like I was writing it from the outside. I ended up not taking the money.

Wes screened Louis Malle's *Murmur of the Heart*. I'd never seen it. At the time I was playing around with ideas for a movie about brothers who were about my age, thinking about their parents' divorce from when they were children. Probably because that's what I was doing at that time—thinking about my childhood. Watching that movie, though, I thought:

Why not come at this from the time it happened? Write about the kids going through it. It wasn't like I ran home that night and hit the keyboard, but somewhere around that time I started writing conversations between two brothers, a 16-year-old and a 12-year-old. Probably six months later I had a rough draft that was pretty connected in spirit to what I ended up shooting four years later.

It was exciting because I felt I'd had a breakthrough. It was the subject matter, the people, the setting and all that stuff, but also just the way I wrote it. I felt like I was more connected to all the characters and in their heads in a way I hadn't felt on previous scripts. I was more open.

Tell me how you start thinking about constructing a character. Is it as deliberate as piecing traits together one by one, or does one start speaking and develop itself from there?

NB: It could go either way. In this case it started with kids not too different from me and my brother. How did we talk? In other cases it might be an exchange I've overheard or invented in my head, and for whatever reason I like the way it sounds

Squid and Whale, however, was always going to deal with the divorce. It wasn't like I started with the characters and said, "Oops, they got divorced!" But generally, in the early going, I try to leave as much open as I can.

The characters you write are generally very flawed people. Do you worry about an audience's empathy?

NB: I hope people will have more empathy for flawed people.

Squid and the Whale *is paced very differently from your past films. Can you tell me how you thought about that, or felt it out?*

NB: That's something that came as I wrote the script and developed even further as I cut the film. In earlier versions of the script, a scene would end, and then there'd be a descriptive line like, "Walt meets eyes with his father. They both look away," or, "He walks out of the room. He looks disappointed." I think the more I got into the material—the more I realized how I didn't need those things. It would be more effective if the movie just kept happening and you didn't have time to reflect. The ending is a moment of stillness and peace, but it's also abrupt. I wanted to leave you suspended.

Is some of that the continued learning process of what screenwriting is? Or, perhaps, just appropriate to this particular story?

NB: Both. The pacing of *Kicking and Screaming* is much different—scenes end about four times. There will be the natural end—when the important dialogue has been covered—there'll be an extra joke, someone will leave the room, someone will be left in the room, and they will do maybe some funny turn of the head after an extended beat. That's more appropriate for that movie because, it's in many ways about how the world doesn't conform to its characters' indulgences. I always liked leaving them with awkward endings. It was about lingering. That said, if I did it now, that movie would be paced differently.

How do you think about a script as a document, in terms of its purpose, and how does that affect what goes on the page? Knowing you're going to direct it, there must be things you feel don't need to be on the page, as opposed to if it's something you're trying to sell.

NB: The problem is that—and this is true if you do or don't direct your own work—if you didn't write it down, there's a good chance it's not going to end up in the movie. But, at the same time, you obviously can't describe everything everyone's wearing or the color of every room, so I think it's sort of instinctual: What feels right for this stage of the movie's development? The more I write, the more that kind of stuff becomes clearer to me earlier on than it used to.

How much rehearsal time did you get with your actors on **Squid and the Whale?**

NB: With the kids it was a longer, more casual process; we'd hang out, but we'd also read the script. I wanted Jessie and Owen to get to know each other. They would trade DVDs and play ping-pong. I had roughly two weeks with Jeff and Laura. It's tricky to rehearse for a film. You want to get it to a point where it's on the verge of something and not any further, because once they nail it and you have to re-create it, you've rehearsed too much. Sometimes the scene goes really well right away, and you don't want to touch it again until you shoot. But we had such a short shooting schedule—23 days—that I knew we needed to work a lot of stuff out in the rehearsal process.

Jeff and I had met two months prior to official rehearsal—we mostly talked about the script and the character. Then he came back from another job, when we were few weeks away from shooting, and we started running scenes. Initially we had some trouble; something wasn't feeling right for him, and I wasn't quite happy. And then we had a breakthrough. After a weekend, he came back and said, "I think I'm doing more of an imitation of what you want, and I think I need to bring more of myself to it." I remember thinking at the moment, "Okay, but I still want what I want." But he started doing it and it made all the difference. We never looked back. I'd had such a specific idea of that character—I would do imitations of it for myself—and he reinvented it. I now do imitations of him. I think a lot of rehearsing, too, is also about getting to know someone and how to talk to them. I want something specific, but I also want something that only they can provide.

Did you see the aesthetic of the film as you were writing it? It was mostly handheld, right, and very different from your past films.

NB: Initially, I thought I was going to have more money to make the film, like six or seven million dollars, but I still wanted to do it with Super 16 and to handhold it. So, fortunately, when we ended up with one and a half million, I had already planned to do it that way, and I wasn't compromising. Neither the director of photography, Robert Yeoman, nor I had shot in Super 16 before, so we had to learn about it. I'd never done handheld in a major way, either, and I suppose if you were looking at my three movies you'd say this was a departure. It's handheld, but very steadily handheld. You can detect a hint of movement. It added to the immediacy of the whole thing.

You tend to bring in things that are familiar and evocative to you during production, like using friends in smaller rolls, and didn't you put Jeff Daniels in your father's clothing?

NB: Yeah, I was thinking about this the other day. It's like when someone goes to work at a new job, and they get to their office or cubicle, and take out things that remind them of home, and start laying them out. For me, during both the writing and directing stage, it's about finding an environment that connects me more strongly to the material.

Some days it doesn't work as well as others and you don't know why. You just can't concentrate. When you're shooting there are so many factors that can take you out of it, and you have to battle. Some days with writing it feels like a real task and other days I feel much more connected.

Well, I guess the last thing is the image of the squid and the whale at the Museum of Natural History, which I remember vividly from my own childhood, as something both terrifying and riveting that my mother would have to pull me away from. Was that something you wanted to use in the beginning or did you find it along the way?

NB: Because it's the title of the movie, I get asked, "Who's the squid? Who's the whale? What does it represent?" All that kind of stuff, which I don't know. I didn't have the location in mind when I started the script. When I was writing the scene with Walt and the school therapist, I got to the point in the dialogue where the shrink asks Walt to think about a nice memory. And the memory was the museum. As a kid, I did love that museum. And I went there with my mother. Ultimately I realized the movie should end there, too. That said, I'm aware it's a provocative, great image, and it's going to take on significance. And if you call the movie that, you're asking for it.

Rob Feld is a writer and independent producer at Manifesto Films. His writings on film and interviews with such noted filmmakers as James Brooks, Charlie Kaufman, Bill Condon, Peter Hedges, and John Turturro appear regularly in *Written By* magazine and *DGA Magazine*, as well as in the Newmarket Shooting Script® series.

CAST AND CREW CREDITS

SAMUEL GOLDWYN FILMS, SONY PICTURES RELEASING
INTERNATIONAL AND DESTINATION FILMS PRESENT
AN ORIGINAL MEDIA AND AMBUSH ENTERTAINMENT PRESENTATION
AN AMERICAN EMPIRICAL/PETER NEWMAN-INTERAL PRODUCTION

A FILM BY NOAH BAUMBACH

THE SQUID AND THE WHALE

JEFF DANIELS   LAURA LINNEY   JESSE EISENBERG   OWEN KLINE
WILLIAM BALDWIN   HALLEY FEIFFER   AND   ANNA PAQUIN

Casting	Production Designer	Executive Producer
DOUGLAS AIBEL	ANNE ROSS	GREG JOHNSON
Music Supervisor	Director of Photography	Producers
RANDALL POSTER	ROBERT YEOMAN, A.S.C.	CHARLIE CORWIN
		CLARA MARKOWICZ
Music by	Co-Producer	
DEAN WAREHAM AND	JENNIFER ROTH	Produced by
BRITTA PHILLIPS		WES ANDERSON
	Executive Producers	PETER NEWMAN
Costume Designer	REVERGE ANSELMO	
AMY WESTCOTT	MIRANDA BAILEY	Written and Directed by
	ANDREW LAUREN	NOAH BAUMBACH
Editor		
TIM STREETO		

Unit Production Managers. . . JENNIFER M. ROTH, HANS GRAFFUNDER
First Assistant Director . . DAVID WECHSLER
Second Assistant Director . . . ERIC YELLIN

Cast
(In Order of Appearance)

Frank Berkman . . . . OWEN KLINE
Bernard Berkman . . . . JEFF DANIELS
Joan Berkman. . . . . . . LAURA LINNEY
Walt Berkman . . . . . . JESSE EISENBERG
Ivan . . . . WILLIAM BALDWIN
Carl. . . . . DAVID BENGER
Lili. . . . . ANNA PAQUIN
Graduate Students . . . . MOLLY BARTON,
BO BERKMAN, MATTHEW KAPLAN,
SIMONE KAPLAN, MATTHEW KIRSCH,
DANIELLA MARKOWICZ, ELIZABETH
MERIWETHER, BEN SCHRANK,
AMY SREBNICK, JOSH SREBNICK,
EMMA STRAUB, ALAN WILKS
Man with Joan. . . . . . JAMES HAMILTON
Otto. . . . . ADAM ROSE

Lance . . . . HENRY GLOVINSKY
Jeffrey . . . . ELI GELB
Sophie Greenberg . . . . HALLEY FEIFFER
Talent Show Judges. . . . WAYNE LAWSON,
MICHAEL SANTIAGO, JUAN
TORRIENTE, PATRICIA TOWERS
Mrs. Greenberg . . . . . PEGGY GORMLEY
Mr. Greenberg . . . . . PETER NEWMAN
Greta Greenberg . . . . . . GRETA KLINE
Professor. . . . . MELISSA MEYER
Student with Puppets . BENJAMIN SMOLEN
Mr. Simic . . . MICHAEL COUNTRYMAN
Pretty Girl . . . ALEXANDRA DADDARIO
Jeb Gelber . . . . NICO BAUMBACH
Ms. Lemon. . . . . MARYANN PLUNKETT
Hector . . . . HECTOR OTERO
School Therapist . . . . KEN LEUNG
Nurse . . . . JO YANG

Camera Operator . . . . . . NILS BENSON
1st Assistant Camera . . STORN PETERSON
2nd Assistant Camera . . . . DOUG KOFSKY
STEPHEN SPEERS
Still Photographer . . . . JAMES HAMILTON

Videographer . . . . . . NICO BAUMBACH
Script Supervisor . . MASSOUMEH EMAMI
Art Director . . . . . JENNIFER DEHGHAN
Costume Supervisor. . . . . LISA MARZOLF
Set Costumer . . MEI LAI HIPPISLEY COXE
Assistant Costume Designer KAREN WAITON
Key Hair Stylist. . . . . . . LORI GUIDROZ
Key Make-up Artist . . . MAYA HARDINGE
Sound Mixer . . . . ALLAN BYER
Boom Operator . . . . . ALFREDO VITERI
Key Grip . . . . BOB ANDRES
Best Boy Grip . . . . . ALLISON BARTON
Grips . . EVELINA ANDRES, GEORGE ELIAS,
IRA PAUL TURNER, BOBBY ANDRES
Gaffer . . . . . DOUGLAS W. SHANNON
Best Boy Electric . . . . JOHN SCHWARTZ
Electricians . . GAY RIEDEL, KEITH KALOHE-
LANI, BERNARD JAMES, SCOTT KINCAID,
SIMEON MOORE, BETH O'BRIEN, CHRIS
HAYES, LISA MARIE GLEESON, SCOTT
MAHER, DAVE RUDOLPH
Production Coordinator . . STEVE KORNACKI
Assistant Production Coordinator . . . .
TODD JUDSON
Production Accountant . . . .
DEIDRE SCHROWANG
1st Assistant Accountant . . JASON R. STANT
Location Manager . . . . . MICHAEL FUCCI
Assistant Location Manager . . KEITH KRINSKY
Property Master . . . . JEFF BUTCHER
First Assistant Props . . . NANCY GRIFFITH
Set Decorator . . . . ROBERT COVELMAN
Leadperson . . . . SUSAN TATOM
On Set Dresser . . . . . JAMES SHERMAN
Assistant Editor . . . . . PERRI B. FRANK
Post Production Supervisor . . . .
CHRIS KENNEALLY
Add'l Post Production Supervisor . . . .
JOE HOBECK
Post Production Accounting . . . .
DEIDRE SCHROWANG
Supervising Sound Editor/Re-recording Mixer. .
LEWIS GOLDSTEIN
Sound Effects Editor. . . . . . MARK FILIP
Dialogue Editor . . . . JULIA SHIRAR
Foley Editor and Recordist . . . .
RACHEL CHANCEY
ADR and Foley Recordist . DAMIAN VOLPE
Foley Artists JAY PECK, SHAUN BRENNAN
Post Production Sound Intern . . . .
DEREK SOMARU
Titles Designed by . . . LEANNE SHAPTON
Camera Scenic . . . MADELINE HARTLING
RICHARD LAURENZI
Transportation Captain . . . . KEVIN FLYNN

Grip and Electric Truck Driver . . JIM KELLY
Key Set Production Assistant . . . . TOM LEE
Assistants for American Empirical . . . .
DANIEL BEERS, LILLIAN PARKER
Assistant to Peter Newman . . . .
CHELSEA HORENSTEIN
Assistant to Andrew Lauren. . . . .
RICHARD BEAVER
Assistant for Original Media . . . .
ALYSON PERLONGO
Casting Associate STEPHANIE HOLBROOK
Extras Casting . . . . . ULYSSES TERRERO,
T & T CASTING
Extras Casting Associate . GIMARDI CUETO
Caterer . . . . ANTHONY TORRE,
GOURMET TO U
Catering Assistant . . . . . ANGELO PINA
Craft Service . . . . . PATRICK MAHONEY
Production Counsel DONNA BASCOM, ESQ.
Financing Counsel . . . . . . FOOTE AND
ASSOCIATES, WALTER FOOTE, ESQ.
Completion Guarantor FILM FINANCES, INC.
Insurance . . . AON/ALBERT G. RUBEN
Payroll Services . . . . . ENTERTAINMENT
PARTNERS, INC.
Production Bank . . CITY NATIONAL BANK
Sales Representation. . GOTHAM SALES, INC.
Art Department Assistants . . . . COSTANZA
THEODOLI, BRASCHI, JASON BRUNO,
BARKER GERARD, LARS LINDHAL,
LAURA NG, MIKE RAISLER, CHARLES
SIEGEL, DAVID WEXLER
Assistant to the Producers . LACEY LEAVITT
Assistant to Mr. Baumbach . . . SUSAN SOH
Camera P.A. . . . . TAYLOR LEVY
Camera/Sound Truck Driver. . JASON BUIM
Locations Assistant . . . . . STACY BISSELL
Office Production Assistants . . . .
SOPHIE KAPLAN, CARLA PISARRO
Prop Truck Driver . . . . . . LOUIS LAPAT
Set Production Assistants . . . . . . MICHAEL
ALTMAN, SANDRA CHWIALKOWSKI,
ERICH EILENBERGER, FELIX
GRISEBACH, GABRIEL KOPLOWITZ,
MARTIN LEICHT, CECILIA MORELLI, ALI
NOROD, OLIVER REFSON, ADAM
SHAKINOVSKY, REBECCA TABER,
GERALD TONNEGIN
Offline Editorial Facility And Audio Post
Services . . . . GOLDCREST
Negative Cutter. . . . . NOELLE PENRAAT
Color Timer. . . . . DAVID PULTZ
Digital Opticals by . . . . DUART DIGITAL,
MARKUS JANNER, JENNIFER
RUSSOMANNO, KEITH YUREVITZ

Dailies Telecine and Color by . . . . DUART
FILM AND VIDEO
Camera and Lighting Equipment. . . . . . .
CAMERA SERVICE CENTER
Additional Music by . . . .
DANIEL ANTONIO SREBNICK
Music Coordinator. . . . . . JIM DUNBAR
Music Clearance . . . .
CHRISTOPHER S. PARKER
Score Mixed by . . . . . DIEGO GARRIDO

BLUE VELVET
Courtesy of MGM CLIP+STILL

THREE'S COMPANY
Courtesy of DLT Entertainment, Ltd.

HEY YOU
Written by Roger Waters
Performed by Pink Floyd
Courtesy of EMI Records
Under license from EMI Film & Television Music

HEY YOU
Written by Roger Waters
Performed by Jesse Eisenberg

INTERMEZZI, OP. 76
Written by Johannes Brahms
Performed by Luba Edlina
Courtesy of Chandos Records Limited

COURTING BLUES
Written and Performed by Bert Jansch
Courtesy of Sanctuary Records Group

LIFE DEPENDS ON LOVE
Written and Performed by Bert Jansch
Courtesy of Sanctuary Records Group

LOVE ON A REAL TRAIN
Written by Christophe Franke, Edgar Froese &
Johannes Schmoelling
Performed by Tangerine Dream
Courtesy of Warner Bros. Pictures Inc.

RUN TO YOU
Written by Bryan Adams & Jim Vallance
Performed by Bryan Adams
Courtesy of A&M Records
Under license from Universal Music Enterprises

BRIGHT NEW YEAR
Written and Performed by Bert Jansch
Courtesy of Sanctuary Records Group

HOLLAND TUNNEL
Written by John E. A. Phillips
Performed by John Phillips
Courtesy of Geffen Records
Under license from Universal Music Enterprises

COME SING ME A HAPPY SONG
TO PROVE WE ALL CAN GET ALONG
THE LUMPY, BUMPY, LONG AND
DUSTY ROAD
Written and Performed by Bert Jansch
Courtesy of Sanctuary Records Group

LULLABY
Written and Performed by
Loudon Wainwright III
Courtesy of Colombia Records
By Arrangement with SONY BMG Music Licensing

HEART LIKE A WHEEL
Written by Anna McGarrigle
Performed by Kate & Anna McGarrigle
Courtesy of Warner Bros. Records Inc.
By arrangement with Warner Strategic
Marketing .

KYRIE
Written by Richard Page, John Lang,
Steve George
Performed by Greta Kline

DRIVE
Written by Ric Ocasek
Performed by The Cars
Courtesy of Elektra Entertainment Group
By Arrangement with Warner Strategic Marketing

LET'S GO
Written by Glenn K. Sybesma &
William J. Clayton
Performed by The Feelies
Courtesy of Pravda Records, Inc.

FIGURE 8
Written by Robert Dorough
Performed by Blossom Dearie
Courtesy of American Broadcasting Music, Inc.

STREET HASSLE
Written and Performed by Lou Reed
Courtesy of The RCA Records Label
By Arrangement with SONY BMG Music Licensing

THE SWIMMING SONG
Written and Performed by
Loudon Wainwright III
Courtesy of Columbis Records
By Arrangement with SONY BMG Music Licensing

Special Thanks:

Jennifer Jason Leigh
Phoebe Cates
Kevin Kline
Laura Durning
Roger Waters
Karen Lauder
Brad Gross
Fred Toczek
Georgia Brown
Michael Cary
Jonathan Baumbach
Annette Grant
Ben Schrank
Molly Barton
Peter Bogdanovich
John Fundus
Howard Michaels
Giovanni, Matteo, Roberto,
Daniele 1, Daniele 2, Carolyn, Doug, Annette,
    Hejay, Joe, Elsa, Daniella and Massimo at
    Bar Pitti
Robert Greenhut
Bonnie Wells-Hlinomaz
Barbara Turner
Patrick Costello
Marion Spiegelman
Roger Arar, Esq.
Phil Scotti
Eric Shonz
Thea Vokins
John Quested
Nick Quested
Jeremy Scott
Tim Spitzer
Michael Harrop
Kevin Ginty
Gunilla Ross
Sofia Coppola
Phillis Lehmer
Maureen Duffy
Amy Rice
Elizabeth Untiedt
Sallie Slate

The American Museum of Natural History
Midwood High School
Brooklyn College
Todtri Book Publishers
F.D.N.Y. at Fort Totten
The Montauk Club
Mayor's Office of Film, Theatre and
    Broadcasting

P.J. Clarke's Restaurant
Hardwick Johnson and Charlie Tammaro
    at Camera Service Center
The Roosevelt Island Racquet Club
DLT Entertainment Ltd.
Film Finances
The Residents of
    Park Slope, Brooklyn

Adidas
Claire's
Clarks
Everlast
Fila
Fossil
Frye
Guess
Jordache
Le Sport Sac
Nike
Northface
O.P.
Puma
Rockport
Saucony
Urban Outfitters

Sheet music permission courtesy of Warner
Bros. Publications (US) Inc.
and International Music Publications Ltd.

BURGER KING drinking glasses and
trademarks used with permission of Burger
King Brands, Inc.

ABOUT THE WRITER/DIRECTOR

Noah Baumbach (Writer/Director) was born and raised in Brooklyn, New York. He wrote and directed the films *Kicking and Screaming* (1995) and *Mr. Jealousy* (1998). He also co-wrote *The Life Aquatic with Steve Zissou* (2004) and the upcoming *The Fantastic Mr. Fox* from a novel by Roald Dahl with Wes Anderson. He is a contributor to *The New Yorker* magazine's "Shouts & Murmurs" department.